CONTENTS

Written and Compiled by Bonnie Canino
Illustrations by Yvonne Reis

2013

About the Author

Her name is **Bonnie Canino.** She has been training and teaching champions, amateur and professional fighters, both male and females since 1979. Through her years as a competitor, she developed superior training methods helping her to achieve "World Champion" status for both, herself and her fighters.

Bonnie competed in 33 Professional Kickboxing fights and 18 Professional Boxing fights. She held two (2) World Championships in kickboxing (K.I.C.K and WAKO) and two (2) World Championships in boxing (WIBF and IFBA). In 1995, she became the first Puerto Rican Female Boxing Featherweight World Boxing Champion.

Her years of Martial arts studies helped her to understand the different styles of boxing. She has learned to train her boxers how to adapt to these styles using various training methods.

When all of her counterparts are writing or have written memoirs about their time as a fighter in and out of the ring, Bonnie's memoirs are a "how to box" book. Well, having the honor of knowing her or when you read any quote she has made throughout the years she always says "I live, eat and sleep boxing", I am not surprised.

So yes, this book and those to follow are Bonnie Canino's memoirs with an occasional water break or rest round where she shares the moments outside of the realm of boxing, yet still in and around the world of boxing.

I remember when we picked up a coach from the airport years ago for the National Women's Golden Gloves Tournament we hosted that year. She asked us, "What do you girls do for fun?" We looked puzzled at each other and said. "We Box."

I hope you enjoy the details and depth of this book as a teaching tool for both stand up fighting and fitness.

Yvonne Reis
Former WBC Middleweight World Champion
(One of hers)

All Style Stand up Fighting-Book I

To perform at your best you must first start at the beginning. One fundamental will lead into another and without one of them you cannot be at your fullest strength. People often ask me: "What makes a Champion?" There are three things in a champion **Body**, **Mind and Soul.** You must put them together within you to become one. Each book will help guide you to understand not only your challenger but it will also help you understand challenges within yourself. As much as fighting is an art it is also a way of life.

Book 1 – The Body -The Physical Preparation.

I dedicate this book to an outstanding Heavyweight Kickboxer with an accomplished record of 22-1 (20 knock outs), **Jimmy Colombo**. He was part of our fighting family, we trained together, fought on the same cards and we traveled together spent countless hours and days chasing our dreams. Jimmy started in 1988 and in April 1993, Jimmy had an accident in the Ring that changed his and all our lives forever. Jimmy is still living in a coma to this day at home. This was the biggest obstacle in my heart, my career, my dream that I had to go through. My words cannot describe this sadness that still cuts my heart for Jimmy. These accidents just don't happen in the ring. They can happen doing anything.

POSITIONING / STANCE

Chapter 1

Knowledge will always give you an advantage but knowing when to use that knowledge is the key to fighting. Position and stance are important but first you must understand it and understand the basics fighting styles. When you are not in the right position you will not have the proper structure or balance to perform at your fullest. A boxing or fighting position is a must to take on your challenger. It will also enable you to be in a defensive position but move into an offensive position quickly. The key to everything is the first subject, your **Positioning and Stance**.

Middle Line / Center Line

First imagine cutting your body in half. This is your center line. Everything taught in this book will revolve around your **center line.** This is the key and the focus point of almost everything you will do.

On the center line there are 2 sides of you: The right side and the left side. Same applies to your opponent. There are positives and negatives about the Center line when facing forward or to the side on your challenger.

Positives:

- You can get from point A to point B faster punching on one center line to the other center line in a straight line.

- You are the strongest on your center line. You can lift a lot more weight using the center of gravity and get maximum strength of leverage.

Negative:

- The most vulnerable parts of your body run on the center line; Examples are your eyes, nose, throat, stomach, groin, knees and feet.

- You're off balance facing front.
- You are a wide target.
- Your reach or range is shorter

Side Position / Side Line View

Positives:

Negatives:

- Balance is better
- You are a narrow/smaller target
- Arm reach is longer
- There are no weak areas exposed
- Side of you can absorb hits

- Your power and leverage is weaker
- No balance when stepping

The goal is to find and play with both sides to have it all and finding out how to balance yourself when boxing or fighting, when you need to have a good fighting/boxing position.

The **Body Zone** is everything within your body area (width) from the center line to the right and left of you. Everything outside of the zone does not concern you when being attacked. If you open up past your body width you will be weak and exposed and vulnerable. You must keep everything within your **body zone** to keep good form, structure and posture.

Find the balanced Position / Fighting Stance

First, take a step forward with your right or left leg, as if you were walking.

Stop and turn your feet and body a little to the side, but still a little to the front. The feet should be positioned with the left foot on the left side from your center line and the right foot on the right side from your center line.

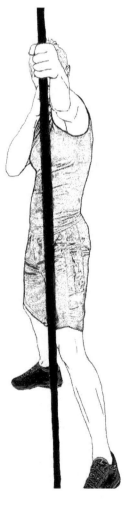

Your feet should **never cross** each other.

The **front foot** should be turned **half way** in the direction towards the center line and **back foot** in the same direction as the front foot also half way allowing you to be able to turn them when you want in either direction. Your feet should be spread **just past shoulder width** with knees slightly bent giving you balance and leverage like a pyramid.

Now, you are not **too** strong or **too** weak **unless** you turn to the front opening up to attack. Remember, when your body turns to the front to attack it is at its strongest. Strike then bring it back to the neutral position or the side position to narrow your target zone and not exposing the weak areas of your body for too long. The goal is to stay balanced and be able to switch positions by turning to the front for offense and to the side for defense and back.

Your **arm position** is in front of your face, facing your opponent. Your lead arm should be **eye level** and a little out from your body. The other arm is in back a little lower, at chin level and closer to you. Both hands ride on your center line. The right hand just a little over on the left side and the left hand a little over on the right side. Like the letter X crossing the center line. Your elbows should not stick out to the side; they stay in your body frame. We call it the **body zone** in this book. Your body is slightly tilted forward for leverage for the arms. Like a stick holding up a wall.

This is called your **Fighting Stance**. In many sports this position may be simpler. Whatever side you want forward is up to you. It is believed that whichever eye sees best put the foot forward or what feels good is what is important.

A Conventional Stance, this is the most frequently used stance. If a person writes with their right hand, they generally put their right leg back to have their strongest hand in a strong position.

The other stance is the **South Paw Stance**. Some boxers like their strong hand in the front in a weak position and their weak hand in the back for a strong position use whatever feels best and most balanced for you. **Do** stay and practice in that one fighting stance position either southpaw or conventional. **Do not;** at the beginning keep switching stances you will confuse your mind and body while developing strategy and proper technique.

Convention

South Paw

How can you find out what Stance is best for you?

1.   If you went to push your car off the road, what foot would you put in front?

2.   Have someone push you which leg steps back?

3.   Close one eye and then the other, what eye sees the best looking forward?

4.   If running a race, which foot would you put back to start?

5.   In tennis what side would you put forward to serve or other sports like basketball, skate board, surfing?

In Chapter 1, you learned about the center line, weak and strong parts of the body, eye focus positioning, center balance, body zone, hand guard position and a boxing/fighting stance.

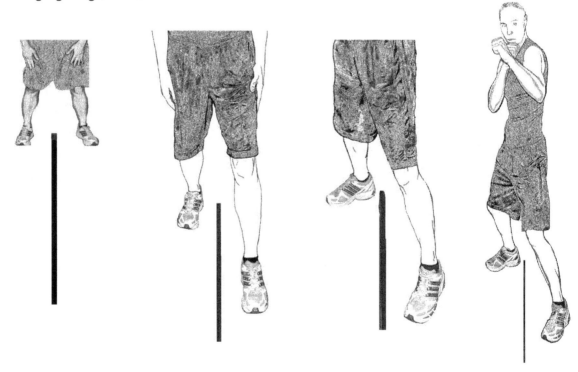

Water Break

A first for Women's boxing WIBF World Titles. WIBF President Barbara
Buttrick and me winning the Featherweight Title in April 1995

In the fight back in 1995, the commentators mentioned what a great set of punches I
threw throughout the entire fight. So, I went back and watched the fight video. I notice the
ripping of the punches meaning one punch followed the other and the sets of punch
combinations I was throwing naturally without realizing it. I thought I should study what I
did to have such quickness between the timing from one punch to another and the sets of
punch combinations thrown. I learned in how to throw them, when to throw them and
practice them over and over so I could be even better in the ring. To this day I can set up
my challengers, execute those punches and remain in good defensive positions at the
same time.

7

<u>HOW TO THROW A PUNCH</u>
<u>TYPES OF PUNCHES</u>

In this chapter, you will learn the how's, why's, when and what kind of punches you can throw to zero in on your target without losing your position and defensive guard. These drills will help you develop good habits.

Making a fist and hitting with it!

Roll your fingers up into a tight ball with your thumb underneath the first two fingers on the outside of your rolled up hand. You strike with the first two biggest front knuckles on your hand closest to your thumb. Your hand should be straight in line with your wrist and forearm with no bend. This is why you wear hand wraps or you see fighters getting their hands taped up protecting the knuckles and wrist.

You should always punch eye level at first aiming your two knuckles like a sight of a gun, rifle or a bow and arrow.

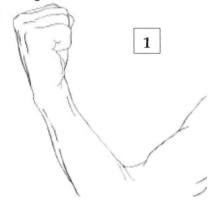

1. Your elbow should be in front of your body, turn your hand so that the palm of your fist is toward your face.

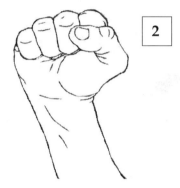

2. Turn fist sideways (vertical) and push the elbow behind the hand about 1" from striking area.

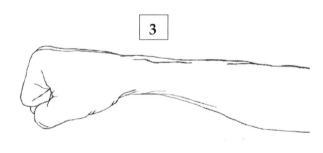

3. Turn the wrist all the way on impact, palm facing down, eye level with the front two knuckles striking precisely the intended target.

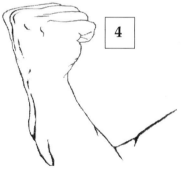

4. Return your fist back to the 1" position then bringing your arm back all the way to the centerline area. You will bring your arm ½ way back sometimes but we will cover why's and when late. Start by bringing the hand back all the way. Practice good habits.

Throwing a Punch

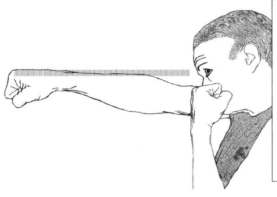

Note: The other hand should be on guard on the center line watching for incoming punches from opponent. Imagine your hand is wearing a helmet on your head like in football. If one hand is playing offense the other hand is playing defense and protecting your body.

It's important practice good Marksman be a sharp shooter when throwing a strike.

A punch needs the shoulder and/or butt or hips behind it to have power. If not then it's an arm punch, which leads to a lot of mistakes.

First, get started practicing how to throw a punch from your fighting position. Practice alternating your punches, the right and left hand. When one hand goes out for the punch while it's returning throw the other punch with the other hand.

They should pass each other, but don't crash or let them run into each other. The hand that just threw the punch is coming back underneath the punch that is being thrown.

Throw the punches eye level on the center line, as if you are holding and aiming with a bow and arrow or a rifle. Be sure the return of the punch back to your face is fast with each punch.

The alternating punches will cross over the center line a <u>little</u> when reaching its target. This provides a better defense against incoming punches or attacks like the letter **X**.

Now, practice turning (pivoting) your hips forward with your punch. The same side of the hand that is throwing will then be the same side one foot will pivot (turn). Do not pick your feet up off the floor, but keep it on the floor when throwing and turning your hip. The other foot stays on the ground where it keeps your body balanced. If you pivot your hips and feet and turn to the front with your body, you will be at your strongest point and still maintain your side position where you will be at your longest reach. By throwing from your centerline to your opponent's centerline, you will reach the shorter distance, a straight line. This will add speed to your punch making it get there faster.

Remember you must keep arms in front of your **Body zone**. Anything outside of it is a waste of time and dangerous and you will not be at your fullest leverage point.

6 – BASIC PUNCHES

Now that you are starting to understand the center line, it's time to learn the variety of punches you can choose and punch with. You have two hands and there are only two ways a punch can come in on you. Either it will be coming straight in from one center line to yours or in a circular motion from one center line to the next. Imagine a knife coming in on you on a straight or circular motion.

The **Lead Jab** and your **Cross punch** are both straight punches from your center line to your opponent opponent's center line.

The **Lead Uppercut** and **Rear Uppercut** are straight punches coming from the center line, but starts from down low and rising up high.

The **Lead Hook** and **Rear Hook** are punches that strike on the sides of your opponent and are considered a circular motion.

The **Lead Jab** is your longest reaching punch and is also your feeler hand. You have been practicing throwing it earlier in this chapter. Now, practice throwing a **double Jab** with your lead hand. Aim on the center line, eye level with your body in the side position fighting stance. Your chin is down a little, hiding on the inside of your shoulder muscles, using it to protect your face when throwing and the other hand is by your face in front on the center line.

Note: When throwing a double Jab **do not** return the first Jab back to the face all the way, only return the first jab half to ¾ quarters of the way back. We will discuss the reasons for this later in the chapter but one of the reasons is when you return your Jab all the way back it will take too long between Jabs.

The **Cross punch** is the rear hand punch. Throw the cross by itself and return it back fast. It has a shorter reach than your jab. Your jab hand hides on your inside shoulder. Try it with the cross for a tighter punch when throwing right down the center line. The **cross** is your **power hand**.

Try the **Jab, Cross** returning back fast to the center line in front of your face. Now **Jab, Cross, Jab, Cross** throwing **four** punches fast, still pivoting the hips, hiding your chin with each punch on the inside of your shoulder and on the center line. Remember your basics from earlier.

UPPERCUTS

An uppercut can be thrown with either hand and is a great strike for a low hit to the stomach, or with a shorter opponent, or if your opponent is coming in with their head down. Uppercuts strike to the body but are mainly used to hit someone in the head or underneath their chin. It also can be used in a combination.

Lead uppercut: This punch is thrown with the body leaning over to the same side as the hand that is throwing the uppercut. Be sure to bend the knees and stay flexible. Keep your body twisted to the side a little (turned). Elbow in front of your hip. Release your hand as you twist back to the middle with the elbow releasing the **uppercut** rising up to the middle (center line) in a vertical upward movement, then twist the punch/ hand (palm facing you) one inch before the striking area. Keeping your elbow behind punch, twist your body and come up, while pivoting the foot that is on the same side of the punch.

Rear Uppercut: Practice alternating throwing the uppercut with the right and left, cross the hands and cross the centerline when one is returning and the other is being thrown as they pass by each other.
Uppercuts are also straight punches coming from the centerline, but coming from down low, rising up high.

LEAD and REAR HOOK

When you think of a hook, think of a fishing hook, or the Pirate Captain Hook's arm you saw in films or pictures or even a baseball bat that swings all the way through.
A hook is a circular punch and comes in from the side of your opponent to the centerline in a circular movement, and then the arm hooks back to you after hitting the target.

The hand is vertical until 1" before impact. Turn your hooking fist inward towards the opposite side with your elbow following through the movement until your fist reaches the center line.
You can also twist your fist like a cross on a hook instead of hooking back into to you. Europeans use this technique a lot.

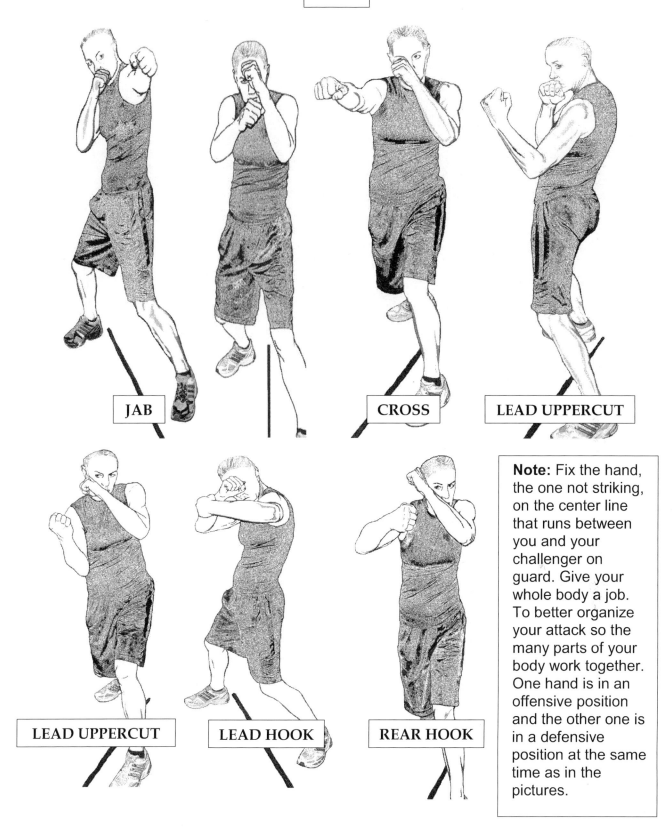

JAB

CROSS

LEAD UPPERCUT

LEAD UPPERCUT

LEAD HOOK

REAR HOOK

Note: Fix the hand, the one not striking, on the center line that runs between you and your challenger on guard. Give your whole body a job. To better organize your attack so the many parts of your body work together. One hand is in an offensive position and the other one is in a defensive position at the same time as in the pictures.

Practice aiming and throwing the punches you just learned on the bag but do not hit the bag. First practice them by placing your punches on the bag making sure your two front knuckles are striking correctly. This helps you feel your structure from the elbow, wrist, hand and when your body is at the right **Range**. The whole fist should land solid and flat, with the weight on the front two knuckles of the fist

Practice this slow at first and without hitting the bag hard. You are just using the bag to judge your distance between you and the bag, place your punches to make sure to feel and see how your hand should land on the bag with the focus on **the front two knuckles and range**.

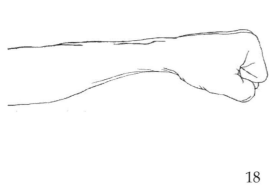

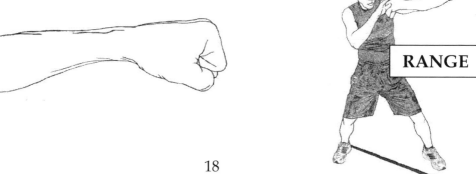

Throw the six varieties of punches as you turn the body while maintaining your stability, balance and structure with your feet and body.

UPPERCUTS   **HOOKS**

Remember that there are two sides to everything. Meaning that the same punches you use to attack are also coming in at you. This is where you focus on your range and defensive posture.

Drill 3

Stand facing front with your feet shoulder width apart.

Practice your **Cross** with each hand while turning side to side keeping you feet shoulder width. This drill helps you get your entire body organized and working together as you pivot and turn from side to side and punch. The other hand is on the center line while pivoting your feet. Practice pivoting and releasing your punch at the same time.

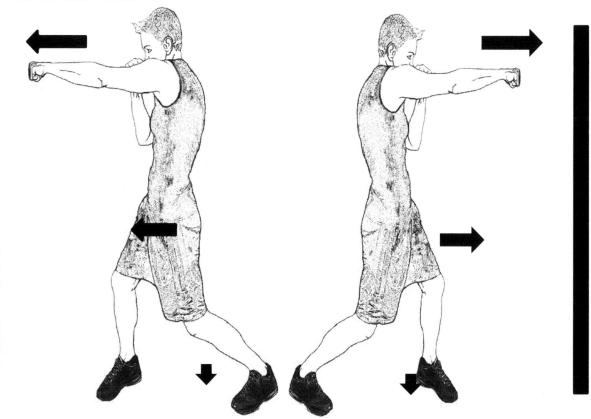

Practice all these drills going from side to side with the punch without stopping, work your cardio exercise of 30 repetitions. Start out with the straight punch.

Practice the same drill with uppercuts, except give a little dipping motion. Work in all you have learned so far in the previous chapters and drills. The most important thing in this drill is the **turning of the body**

Practice your Hooks by imagining the challenger is in front of you. **Don't worry** about your fighting position. You are learning to turn the body while punching and manitaining your balance. You first need to get the feel the motion.

Throw three straight punches then turn to the other side and throw three straight punches. Be fluid when throwing your punches. Be sure that as one hand comes in while the other is going out. A slight pivot with your hips and feet are recomended.

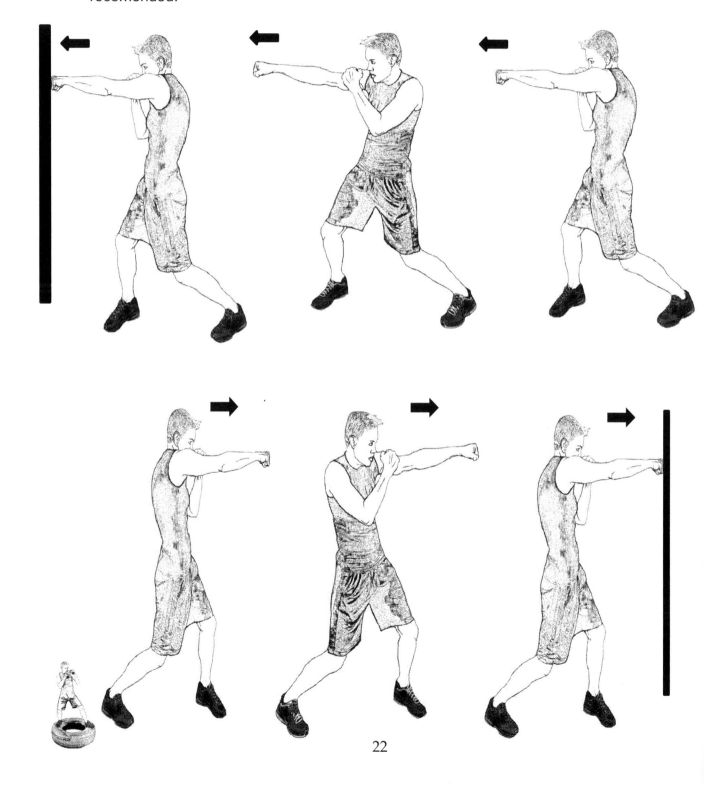

This time try to roll three uppercuts going to the right side then three upppercuts to the left side. Counting each side to keep in rhythm.

My punch combinations played a role in winning my IFBA World Title fight in1997. This world title fight was against Beverly Symanski. I couldn't do any wrong until the last two rounds. I got mentally bored using the same method that had me winning the fight so why change. I found myself making a few more mistakes and leaving myself open more. Now I was taking a few more punches than I had in the earlier rounds which made it more intense for my corner and me. I had to pull myself through those last two rounds to walk out with another World Title. That month I received the boxer of the month award. My combinations did come out with all the practice at the gym. I kept using them during fights when the opportunity arose. I learned every day is different and what works with one challenger might not work as well with another one.

Me, Bert Rodrigues, Jimmy Columbo and David Vander Hee, Ft. Lauderdale Beach in 1992. These guys helped me win my Championship fights from 1988 to 1993.

Double Hooks

Try doubling the hook. First punch low crunching down to hit the body. Pull back the punch half way and release the second hook to the face twisting while coming up from your crunch to the other side. Be sure to set up the attack to throw the low hook to the other side with the other hand. Remember to get the feel of your body in motion while twisting.

This concludes this chapter on throwing punches and drills to smooth out your team assign jobs to your whole body.Repeat the drills over and over to get the feeling. **Watch yourself in the mirror to see if your hands are up. If you can see yourself clearly in the mirror, so can your challenger. If your hands and arms are up where you can not see your face clearly then you are correct and your hands are good. This is what your challenger sees.**

In the corner

A Summary of Highlights – When the fighter comes to the corner between rounds, the trainer reminds them of their drills, recommends combinations etc. so in summary…

1. Center line
2. Throwing the punch just over to the other side of the centerline.
3. Aiming.
4. Crossing your punches over or under the other punch as it rotates to throw again.
5. Throwing punches eye level and having the other hand up on the centerline for guard against incoming punches.
6. Keeping a distance between you and your challenger (bag) when throwing a punch and not to crowd yourself.
7. Twisting and turning with the punch.

Moving and Shadow Boxing

27

This chapter explains **Shadow Boxing**. It is important because it works the basic understanding of foot work and timing your punches and feet together. Both feet must be on the floor to stay **grounded** and be in **balance** before impact so your hard punch is at its fullest power. You must learn how to put the final impact of the punch behind it with the upper torso (**shoulder**) or the lower torso (**butt**) to be at fullest power. Enabling you to step in different directions you need to give job assignments to your whole team (body parts) to work together. Getting and keeping rhythm with your whole body involved move around like you are fighting an imagined challenger in front of you.

Note: Always keep your feet spread wide, just past shoulder width even when you are dancing around.

Drills are important to practice, to get the feeling and experience without having the contact.

The rule is that your feet should be planted on the impact of the punch to get the full power. So if you are moving around you need to come to a standstill for a second when you connect. In this drill you practice timing your feet with your punches working together as one unit. If you make the sound of a stomp with one foot at a time with your foot, feel the connection of stopping, balance, timing, positioning and the power of the punch. As you progress, stop making the sound of a stomp.

Practice picking your foot up slightly and stepping straight down with each punch in your fighting position. Let's start with your lead hand.   Throw the **Jab** and with your lead foot (the right) pick it up slightly and make a stomping sound while your left foot stays down (illustrated below) with the jab hitting at its peak of the strike at the same time. Remember you want to hear it land, STOMP. If you don't hear it with your ears you will miss getting the feeling of it.

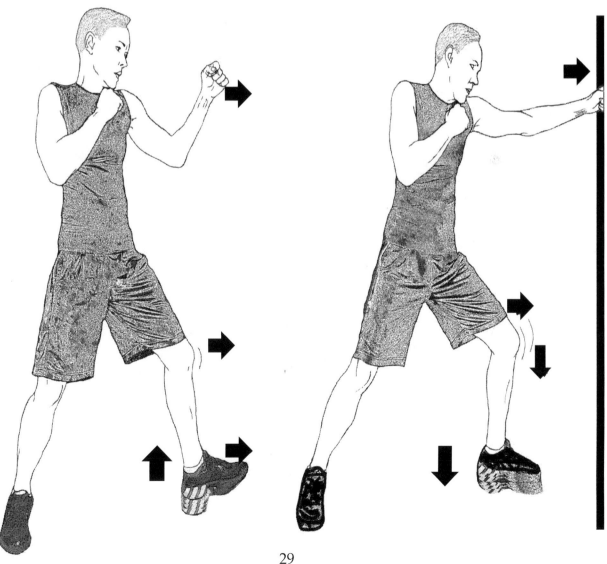

Stomp with the right foot down when punching with right hand a **straight** while remaining in your fighting position. Make sure you make a stomping sound so you can hear the timing of the hand and feet working together. This will help you catch the feeling and balance of the position and power in the punch. Practice your straight punches at first. Once you get the idea try all six punches described in Chapter 2.

Stomp with the right foot down when punching with right hand **straight** while remaining in your fighting position. Make sure you make a stomping sound so you can hear the timing of the hand and feet working together. This will help you catch the feeling and balance of the position and power in the punch. Practice your straight punches at first. Once you get the idea try all six punches described in Chapter 2.

Practice stepping while taking baby steps forward applying the same technique. When you are stomping with your front foot, turn your foot to adjust your pivoting position with your hips when throwing your punch. Make sure your whole foot stomps the ground. Do not bring your foot high when stomping to help you step forward easily.

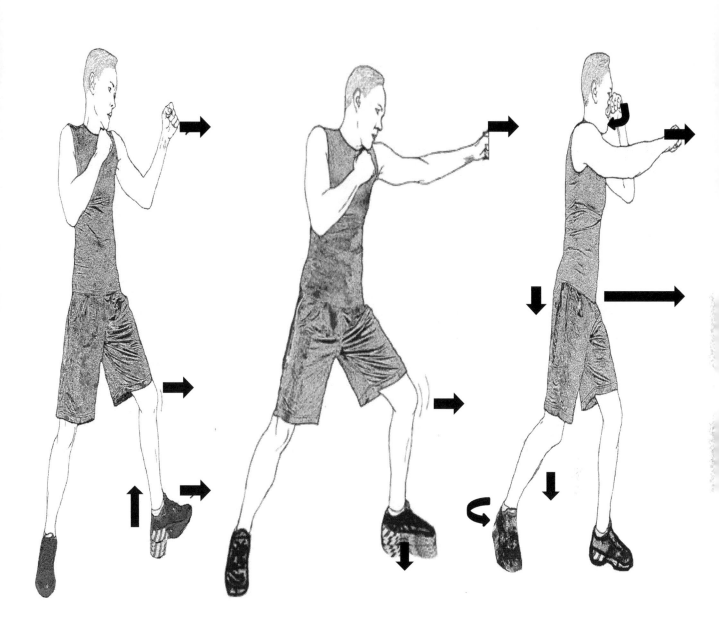

Do not bring your feet together when punching. **Always** keep your feet in your fighting position. Just learn to turn your hips or lean forward a little on the front foot but do not let your head fall forward.

NOTE: Your head should never pass your front knee. If it does you are leaning in.

Once you have the hang of it, practice this drill with all six punches described in Chapter 2. Your **Jab, Cross, Uppercuts, and Hooks**. Master this so you can move forward to the upcoming drills.

I trained for hours and hours when others weren't around or they faded out within an hour. I just kept training. We would run 6 miles at the hottest time of the day, and then jump into a lake that had snakes and alligators in it. We live in Everglades land and Gators are known to hop into lakes. We would swim a 1/2 mile across to the other side and back when finished, I still wanted to keep going.

32

Moving and Stepping; Place four cones in a large square representing four walls. Practice in your fighting stance and keep the front wall as your focus point throughout the drill. This drill goes over how to step and slide your feet to the right and left, forward and back without losing your stance. Move by stepping like an inch worm with small steps in the beginning as you do this drill. Do not cross your feet and always keep to the side position in your fighting stance.

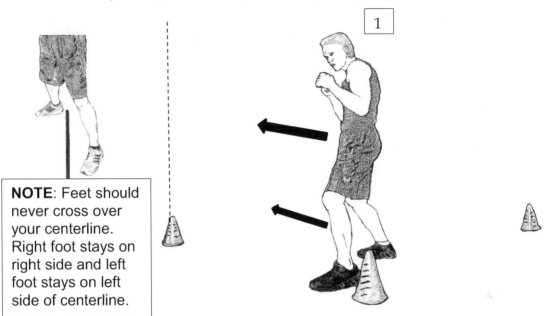

NOTE: Feet should never cross over your centerline. Right foot stays on right side and left foot stays on left side of centerline.

At first do not throw any punches, just concentrate on the feet and in how they are moving. You will move from one cone over to the other cone, then to the back cone, then over to the other back cone and then up to the front cone, where you started, as shown in the illustrations.

In image 1; right foot steps first over to the side, in image 2; your left foot does catch up.

NOTE: A common foot work rule is that the side you are moving too will be with the same foot that moves first. If you are moving to the right side your right foot steps first to the right, then left foot plays catch up.

When moving backwards use the back leg to steps back and the front foot plays catch up back to the fighting position. The foot that plays catch up is also used as a push off foot for a quick getaway.

If you are moving to your left side, step to the left side first and your right foot will play catch up see image 4 below.

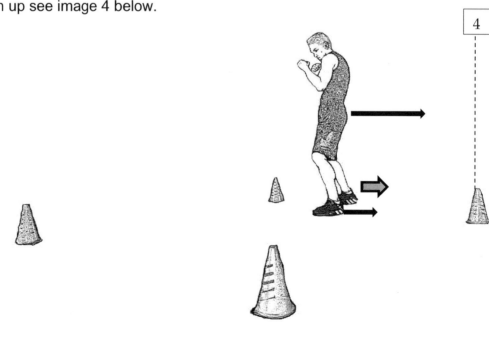

When moving forward your lead left foot shown in image 5 as a conventional stance, steps forward while the back foot plays catch up to the neutral fighting stance.

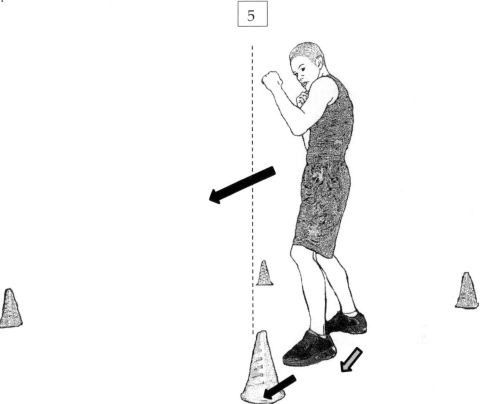

5

By giving your feet a job assigment they will be more fuctionable for you and be organized. Practice this drill as shown in the 5 illustrations moving around to all four cones. Start slow at first before picking it up to a faster rhythm.

Note: Know which foot is stepping and which foot is pushing off but both feet will play both roles. It depends on which direction you are going. The timing with your step and push off foot also matters.

Now work the stomping and your punches with your movement going to the sides, backwards and forwards. Practice that inch worm stepping but add the stomping with the punch as you move from cone to cone as shown in the illustrations.   It is very important to listen for the sound of the stomping and timing the landing of the punch together but moving now.

By putting drill 1, the stomping with your six punches with drill 2, the stepping or sliding in the 4 different directions, you are working what you learned in the previous chapters. This helps later when a challenger is in front you. You will know how to step with your challenger without falling off balance and keeping your center line safe.

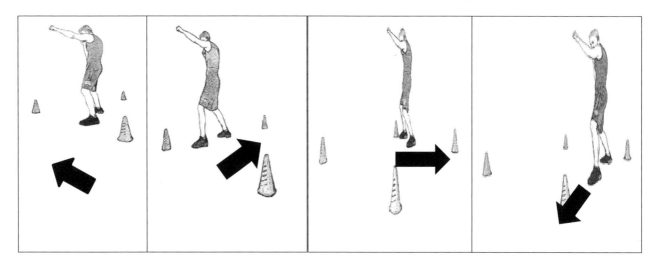

There will be some adjusting to be made with each different punch you throw.   In the illusrtation, you step with the right foot forward while throwing your punch, stomping down as you step into fighting position.

The same rules apply. Right foot, right side, right foot stomps, right punch. Left foot, left side, left stomp and left punch. Right foot stays on the right side of your center line and the left foot stays on the left side of your body's center line, never crossing over your center line with your foot to the other side.

At times most of the guys I had a chance to practice with were always bigger than me. I felt like a feather but once I started to get my timing down with my stepping and punch together I had more power. When the big guys started bulling there way forward in on me, I started to catch their punches in midair. Now having the right balance, I would drop a punch down on them and sometimes drop them to the ground or stopping them in their tracks so they couldn't or wouldn't come in without knowing they might receive a solid punch.

1987 Coco Beach celebrating all of our victories
The crew Bernie, Terry, Michael, Me, Bert, unknown, and John

Let's work on rhythm with a bounce and the movement of the feet. To get a rhythmic bounce first, get a truck tire. Stand on the tire in your fighting stance, feet spread shoulder width apart. Keep your **feet on the tire**; don't let them come off at any time. You don't want to fall off the tire and break your ankle. The higher you bring your feet of the ground the more you will be off balance. Practice with a small rhythm bouncing forward and back. First get in the groove. The rhythm is with the body and legs shifting your body weight to the front leg to the back leg.

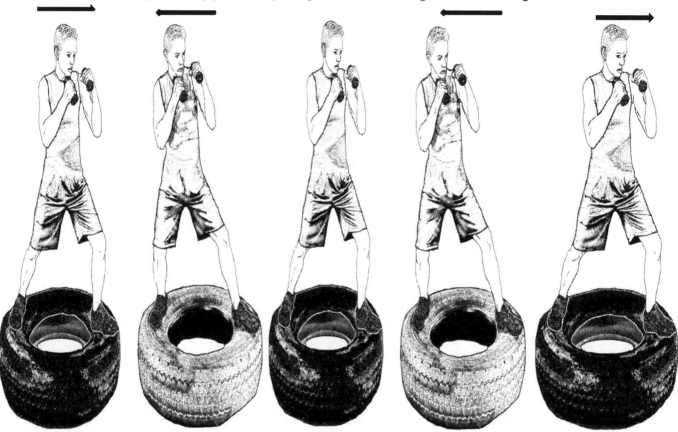

Practice getting the feeling, the groove and beat of shifting forward and back. This will help with your rhythm and timing. Spend a few minutes on just working shifting forward and back with the legs and bouncing in rhythm.

Note: The fighting stance your are in when your leaning back is called a back stance. Your weight is shifted back and a forward stance is when your weight is shifted forward. Compare them to the neurtal fighting stance where your weighis distributed evenly in both legs.

Now throw your jab everytime you lean or shift forward as illustrated below. Remember to still keep the rhythm of moving forward and back and keep both feet on the tire.

Try a cross punch in rhythm when shifting your weight forward.

Start getting the rhythmic bounce, then throw the one, two punch (Jab, Cross) keeping in the beat then get right back into the rhythmic bounce. This drill works on not allowing the challenger to time you. Be random so you do not show when you are going to throw your punch. Illustrations below.

Try more than the one, two, add a lead hook when you shifted the weight to the back leg on the tire below. Fall back into the rhythmic bounce after your combination not to let your challenger know when you are going to throw

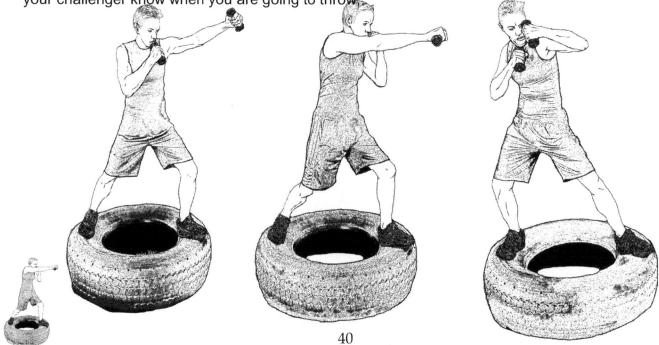

Once you get the hang of it, try adding in some of the punch combinations taught in the next Chapter 4. Below demonstrates throwing a rear uppercut followed by a lead hook.

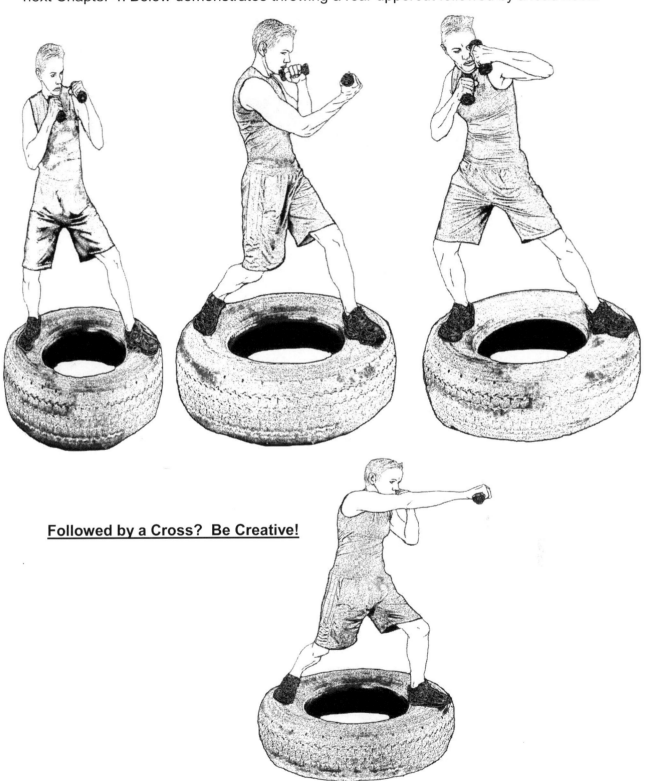

<u>Followed by a Cross? Be Creative!</u>

Place your jump rope or an object in front of you in the form of a circle. Now, imagine your challenger standing in front of you inside the circle. Practice the small rhythmic bounce but this time without the tire to help. Stay in your fighting position, keeping your feet spread wide. Practice a flowing around the circle till moving at ease. Go to the right. Go to the left. Move forward and back keeping the rhythm without your feet crossing over each other.

Shadow box, this time instead of a square with the four cones go around the circle, use the same methods as the previous rounds of shadow boxing; the stepping forward (in), backward (out), to the right and left.

Throw your punches to the middle of the circle which represents your challenger. Use the stomping sound at first to teach yourself to be grounded with the feet and body when punching. Move circling around the rope. Then repeat stepping in, stopping and throwing.

Now, put it all together. Keep both the fighting position and feet **solidly down** on the floor when the punch hits. Reference the **stomping** as in Drill 1. **Move your feet** in the different directions. Practice how to step without losing your fighting position. Getting a **rhythmic bounce** to get a beat/pace helps to keep moving in a way you won't be so stiff or slow to take off. **Moving around the circle** which represents your challenger teaches how to circle around your challenger and not be in their target zone, but for you to be in your target range.

In the corner

So far you have learned how to shadow box while moving your feet by themselves in all directions without losing your position in your boxing/fighting stance. Review keeping a bounce or rhythm, for a quicker take off, while having your feet planted when throwing a punch. In boxing terms it is called being **grounded**. Remember, the punch has to have the shoulder or butt behind it to have power. Practicing these drills and techniques will help you find your timing and balance so you can feel comfortable before you move forward to the next chapter. You should be combining all the chapter drills (1 and 2 with chapter 3) together before moving forward.

The most important thing when you start to shadow box is watch yourself in the mirror. Make sure every part of your body is doing their job. Look at yourself. If you can see your face clearly in the mirror, so can your challenger, which means your hands/arms are not up. Later you want to visualize your challenger in front of you without watching yourself in the mirror.

PUT IT ALL TOGETHER

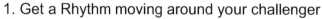

1. Get a Rhythm moving around your challenger
2. Circle to the right or the left
3. Steppng in to punch muting feet grounded when punching –stomping
4. Challenger in on center line. Throw your punches on the center line.
5. Having one hand offense and one hand defense on the center line.
6. One hand goes out the other hand in and tight.
7. One hand should cover high and the other one hand covering low.

Punch Combinations

In this chapter you learn how to use the six punches together in a combination. There are a variety of punch combinations to learn.

Combinations are a series of three, four or more punches combined together in a sequence and rhythm thrown at the challenger. If you were going to war, you need to know different methods of attacking to get in and surprise the enemy. Punch combinations are your dictionary of different series of punches used to attack. Start with these combinations but later you will find your own combinations and add to your own dictionary. With experience these combinations will come out naturally. Throwing one or two punches won't get in on the experienced fighters. The more you practice the more it will come out naturally in good form, fast and strong.

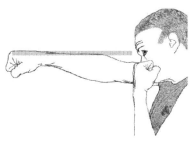

Remember all punches should be thrown on the center line, aimed eye level and each punch should pass by and cross over the other punch being thrown in a combination.

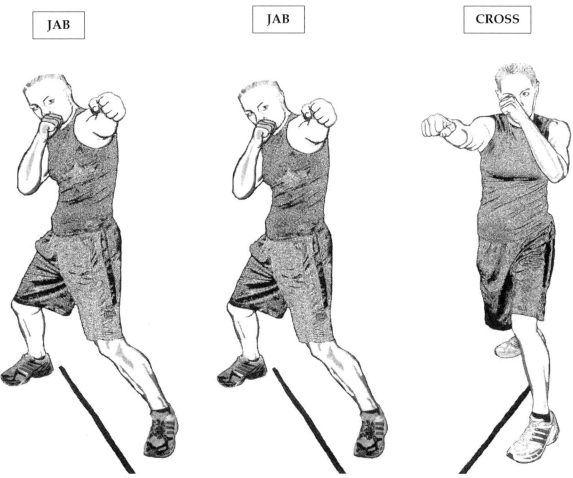

| JAB | JAB | CROSS |

Jab, Jab, Cross

In this combination, your jab does not need to come back to your face all the way to throw it again. Throw a full jab, return it ½ way then pump the fist back out. This is a good attack because it has speed and is straight down the middle on the center line. This is a quick approach method to get in on the challenger if they are sitting back. Practice stomping with each punch in the combination to get the feeling of being grounded and in balance with your feet with each strike.

Make sure you get each hand to do its job. One hand is on offense while the other hand is defense. Don't forget to crisscrosing with the punches in a combination. When one is going out, the other hand is coming back crossing (meeting) in the middle as they pass by.

JAB

CROSS

JAB

CROSS

Jab, Cross, Jab, Cross

JAB

CROSS

CROSS

Note: Incorporate musicial rhythms (a half beat and a full beat) in with your rhythm and timing your movement and punches.

The second cross is pulled back all the way and thrown again.

Jab, Cross, Cross

Here is a great combination. Throw two straight punches then a hook which comes in a circular motion catching your challenger off guard.

JAB

CROSS

HOOK

Jab, Cross, Lead Hook

JAB

HOOK

CROSS

This is a good combination to use when your jab is knocked down.

Jab, Lead Hook, Cross

48

The uppercut punch is hardly ever used, but it's a good sneak attack undeneath and between the chanllenger arms and hands. You hit many different directions on the attack with this combination.

JAB   UPPERCUT   HOOK   CROSS

Jab, Uppercut, Lead Hook, Cross

Attacking under and straight in, with the hook high to the head coming in on the side is a great combinations when youe are fighting in close.

UPPERCUT

UPPERCUT

HOOK

Lead Uppercut, Uppercut, Lead Hook

HOOK

HOOK

HOOK

This attack generates a lot of butt / hip power momentum.

Lead Hook, Hook, lead Hook

.
The lead uppercut is another punch that is not used a lot. But it is a good surprise attack to an unexpected area.

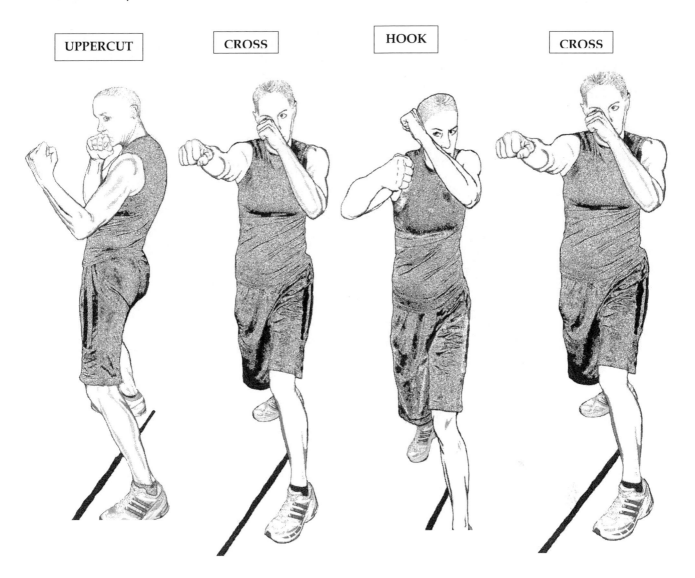

UPPERCUT   **CROSS**   **HOOK**   **CROSS**

Lead Uppercut, Cross, Lead Hook, Cross

If the first or second punch doesn't land, no worries it will open up other areas for the third or fourth punch to land.

1994 Title Fight at the Taj Mahal against Lisa Howarth from England.

In the corner

Every combination will have its own time to be thrown. Later you will have a good library of attacks that you can refer back to. Take the punch combinations you've just learned and repeat them with the movements from **Chapter 3.**

Remember when throwing a combination, it is a set of punches that are rapidly following each other until the end of the combination. There should be a flow from one punch to other. Single jabs, double jabs and triple jabs are good punches to set your challenger up for a combination. The timing in-between the punches will be practiced in the next chapter.

A good smart fighter will have multiple ways to enter and attack. In fighting, sometimes you will just fight free style (with no mind) and hope that what you have practiced shows up. Sometimes, there will be times when you need to think and choose an entry of attack with a combination.

Basic Heavy Bag Training

Basic Heavy Bag 1

Ripping... 2

Snapping/Popping... 3

LADBROKES CASINO SAN PABLO & IN SYNC PRODUCTIONS PRESENT

Budweiser KING OF BEERS   **Budweiser** KING OF BEERS

World Championship

KICKBOXING

VS

WKA & ISKA WORLD CHAMPION
BRIDGETT "BABY DOLL"
RILEY

WAKO & WIBF WORLD CHAMPION
BONNIE "THE COBRA"
CANINO

IKKC & IFCA WOMEN'S JR. FEATHERWEIGHT
WORLD CHAMPIONSHIP TITLE BOUT

Plus 5 Bouts With The Bay Area's
Finest Fighters Including:

Ronnie Wells   Christine Dupree   Mike Tabusco

IKKC JR. LIGHTWEIGHT
WORLD CHAMPIONSHIP TITLE BOUT

IFCA LIGHTHEAVYWEIGHT
NORTH AMERICAN TITLE BOUT

#1 RANKED CONTENDER
BILAM NESRADINE
VS
THREE TIME WORLD CHAMPION
LAWRENCE MIERA

SPECIAL ADDED ATTRACTION:
GEORGE TSUTSUI **VS** **FREDDY MADRANO**

IKKC CHAMPION
ERIC YANEZ
VS
MUAY TRAI CHAMPION
MAURICE TRAVIS

SATURDAY JUNE 22, 1996 7:00 P.M.

(Door opens at 6:30 p.m.)

WORLD CHAMPIONSHIP KICKBOXING

International Karate Kickboxing Council

CASINO SAN PABLO
WHERE WINNERS PLAY
13255 San Pablo Ave., San Pablo, CA 94806   Tel: 510/215-7888

I.F.C.A.

TICKET OUTLETS: LADBROKES CASINO SAN PABLO GIFT SHOP (510)215-7888 * EDDIE SOLIS KARATE KUNG FU, 1169 23RD ST., SAN PABLO, (510)235-6565 * WOLF KEMPO KARATE, 425 APPIAN WAY, EL SOBRANTE, (510)222-6678 * RICK ALEMANY KARATE SCHOOL, 1933 IRVING, SAN FRANCISCO, (415)665-3848 * TAT WONG CALIFORNIA MARTIAL ARTS ACADEMY, 2901 CLEMENT ST., SAN FRANCISCO, (415)752-5555 * MARTIAL ARTS ENTERPRISES, 2123 JUNIPERO SERRA BLVD., DALY CITY, (415)994-5025 * TAT WONG CALIFORNIA MARTIAL ARTS ACADEMY, 53 43RD AVE., SAN MATEO, (415)341-9292 * CLOVERDALE KARATE CENTER, 123 E. FIRST ST., CLOVERDALE, (707)894-9552 * SONOMA COUNTY MARTIAL ARTS CENTER, 5675 REDWOOD DR., ROHNERT PARK, (707)584-3812 * SONOMA COUNTY MARTIAL ARTS CENTER-PETALUMA, 149 KENTUCKY ST., PETALUMA, (707)765-2763
CHARGE BY PHONE: (310)985-3088 * $100 RINGSIDE * $25 RINGSIDE PAVILION * $20 GENERAL ADMISSION

ALL FIGHTS SUBJECT TO CHANGE. Management reserves the right to cancel or modify event at its sole discretion.

55

Basic Heavy Bag Training

In this chapter, you will learn how to connect with your punches without hitting another person.

The bag work training is do at two different distances, a long distance range and a shorter range. The longer range is normally referred to as the **boxer.** A shorter distance is called the **fighter.**

Heavy bag training is a boxer's weight training program. If you want to become a body builder, you lift weights. If you want to become a boxer, you do bag work for weight training.

Heavy bag work helps to develop punching power and strength. The bag represents your challenger in a fight, except, the bag does not think or hit back.

You will learn two ways to put the power behind your punches in the next two chapters. The first rule to generate power in a punch is to have the shoulder or butt behind the strike. These bag drills will help you a feel on how to prepare yourself to attack and stay in good position.

Learn to balance the bag first with your both hands on the bag in fists. This helps you to aim, hit with the right part of the hand and practice good habits. This drill helps to build arm strength and durance.

Place an "X" on the bag with tape

Stand in front of the bag. Push and hold the bag out in a straight upward angle with arms as far as the bag can go out, keeping both hands in fists. The main pressure is on your front two knuckles and your hands are at eye level. The bag should not move around. Don't drop your arms when you get tired. Keep the balance of the bag. If you lose control of the bag, quickly place both hands back on the bags. This exercise makes your hands stay up strong, and promotes good body structure. Try not move around. You are working at your longest distance. Work this routine for a round at two or three minutes duration per round.

Drill 2

Start by holding the bag out with one hand in a fist instead of both and balance the weight on that one hand. Replace the fist with the other hand on the bag before the other punch goes back on defense on the center line. Do not rush. Keep the bag out at the angle for the whole round, trying not to let it move at all.

Practice your straight punches at first. When one hand leaves, the other one is there to replace it. Keep switching hands, start slow. There is no time when a punch is not on the bag for the whole round.

Note: the weight is forward on the lead leg during this drill.

Now increase the speed by reducing the time between each strike.

This drill helps you see what each hand is doing when striking. Make sure you are practicing good habits. Check your fighting stance, position and balance.

This was my third World Title defense in 1993 within 3 months of winning the title.

This next drill is similar to drill 2, but this time you are going to **rip** your punches. Instead of throwing single punches, throw four or five punches fast. Replacing each punch with the other one fast and leaving little to no time in between punches. The other punch returns back for defense to the center line. The bag should not move. One hand should always be on the bag for the round.

Keep exchanging your punches on the bag switching off fast, while holding the bag out. This way you will see what each hand is doing. Make sure you are in a good fighting stance. Practice this drill for two or three round before moving on. Notice the speed you have when you rip those punches on the bag. When ripping, you might not need to bring those punches back all the way to you sometimes ½ way or ¼ way back can be used.

Change the speed of your punches. Throwing fast and then slow changing the rhythm. Throw high to the head and then low to the body, keeping your balance and stance.

Next, move bag move around, while you're holding it out. Adjust your feet accordingly to keep your position. Drop your body weight forward when throwing your punches. Your head never passes your lead knee. Do not fall forward with your head. Look forward.

Add in all the various punches like uppercuts and hooks working a little angle into the movement of your upper body.

Be sure when you are ripping three to four punches not to let the bag move you back. If your punches are thrown correctly, they will land solid and firm on the bag. **Most important is Hit the "X" and keep your eyes on the "X" as a focal point on the bag.**

My first loss was against one of the best known woman fighters in the world Lucia Ricker (18-0 with 18 KOs). I was the first ever to go the distance with her and lost by decision. My next fight was a 12 round World Title Kickboxing fight at Caesar's Palace in Las Vegas with Kathy Long. I received my 2nd lost. It taught me lesson.

I wanted to win so bad after my defeat in Holland, there was nothing that was going to stand in my way. I had too much aggression that fight. It made it easier for my challenger to read me. The harder I tried to attack, to finish my challenger; the more jammed up I got. I became slow and sloppy. I overwhelmed my challenger with force but I didn't win on the Judge's score cards and received a controversial lost. After that fight I got a lot of recognition through media and the fight community. I took that experience and improved on my attack and long range punching. After that fight, my fighting career was on full force.

WCCK

KICKBOXING EXPLOSION: The Beginning
Caesars Palace • Las Vegas   July 7, 1990

Order of Events

Super Welterweight — 6 Rounds

RICKY O'KANE	ALBERTO GARCIA
Los Angeles	Sante Fe, N.M.
16-2-1, 12 KOs	23-2, 17 KOs
Intercontinental Champion	No. 6 Middleweight

Lightweight — 6 Rounds

JUAN TORRES	VICTOR SOLIER
So. Lake Tahoe, Nev.	Silverdale, Wash.
20-2, 10 KOs	21-2, 16 KOs
North American Champion	No. 3 Lightweight

Featherweight — 6 Rounds

LAWRENCE MIERA	DAVID HAMILTON
Albuquerque, N.M.	Greenville, N.C.
23-1, 15 KOs	21-7-1, 10KOs
Intercontinental Champion	U.S. Champion

Super Heavyweight — 6 Rounds

STAN LONGINIDIS	DALE BROUSSARD
Melbourne, Australia	Springfield, MO
14-0-1, 10 KOs	10-0, 8 KOs
Intercontinental Champion	No. 5 Super Heavyweight

Super Lightweight — 6 Rounds

BRIAN DORSEY	KERRY DYE
Dallas, Tex.	Nashville, Tenn.
15-4, 9 KOs	21-8, 8 KOs
U.S. Champion	No. 4 Super Lightweight

WORLD FEATHERWEIGHT CHAMPIONSHIP — 12 Rounds

KATHY LONG	BONNIE CANINO
Bakersfield, Calif.	Miami, Fla.
11-1-1, 5 KOs	11-1, 6 KOs
North American Champion	U.S. Champion

INTERCONTINENTAL WORLD LIGHT HEAVYWEIGHT CHAMPIONSHIP — 12 Rounds

MAREK PIOTROWSKI	TOMMY RICHARDSON
Warsaw, Poland	Jacksonville, Fla.
25-0, 16 KOs	20-7, 20 KOs
Intercontinental World Light Heavyweight Champion	No. 3 Light Heavyweight

INTERCONTINENTAL WORLD SUPER LIGHTWEIGHT CHAMPIONSHIP — 12 Rounds

PETER CUNNINGHAM	LAFAYETTE LAWSON
Edmonton, Alberta, Canada	Hot Springs, Ark.
40-0-1, 18 KOs	30-10, 22 KOs
Intercontinental World Super Lightweight Champion	North American Super Lightweight Champion

Learning to snap/pop your punches

This will help you to understand how to throw a snapping or pop to your punch. An example of a snap or pop, imagine a bull whip striking at the end of its rope as it strikes and returns fast.

First give your whole body job assignments. For this punch we will practice using your shoulders behind the punches. You will learn to measure each punch at your longest range giving distance between you and your challenger.
Focus on the center of the "X" on the bag. Be a sharp shooter when punching. Focus your eye and thought with your front two knuckles on the "X" when punching.

You are not ripping your punches but making sure each punch hits a fraction of a second apart from each other. There is very little time in-between punches and hitting the target. The punches pass by each other at the middle range. When one hand is returning, the other hand goes out for an attack, alternating hands. Roll each punch by the other in a rhythm to help with timing, speed and a popping, snapping motion with your shoulder and body. Stay tight, working the in and out range effectively while shifting the weight of your body when striking and not striking. You are trying to resemble a boxer's look. Reference the tire bounce.

Try to get a rhythm by getting your shoulders to roll one after another with your punches. Keep your feet spread and stay in your boxing stance.

Start with one hand high and out a little out more than the other one which is close to your body on your center line. Crisscrossing your hands in a rolling action. Stay tight, elbows in. Shift your weight forward and back as you move your hands rolling by each other.

Don't let the bag move around at first or on this drill.

Do not move your feet yet and keep a long range between you and the bag. Stay tight and ride the center line with both hands. This is going to help you with speed and to get a snap/pop in your punches when thrown. Once you got the feel of the motion go to the next drill.

Crisscrosing and roll the hands twice and then throw the **jab** by itself.

Now practice crisscrosiing / rolling the hand twice, and then throw the **cross** by itself.

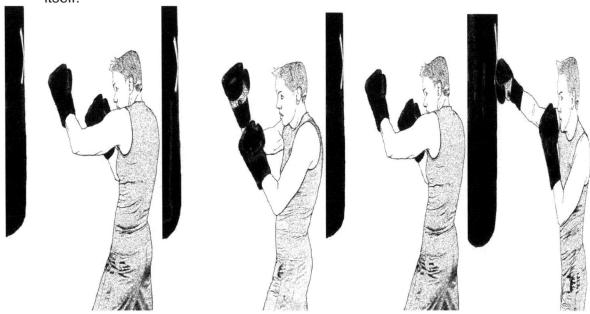

Start out crisscrossing and rolling your hands then throw a **double Jab.**. Practice bringing your punch back fast into guard on the center line. Do not leave you hand out or you will not get a snap or a popping to your punch.

Listen for the popping sound when you hit the bag.

Drill 11

Now throw a **Jab** and a **Cross.** They pass mid range, as the jab is coming back, the cross is going out. The hands should pass by each other in a timing fashion. Make sure the hand that is not punching is on guard on your center line. Bring your punches back fast, setting up your fighting stance and keep a rhythm.

Once you feel the snap and your hands are working together, throw four to five straight punches one right after the other. Throw fast with very little time in-between the punches while crisscrossing and rolling.

Make sure you are at your **longest range** and you are **not crowding** yourself on the bag. Every body part has a job assignments: your hands, feet, etc. Breath out with each punch either out through you nose or your mouth. Sometimes making a poping sound can help. Your eyes are focus on the "X". Sharp shoot your punches on the "X", shifting body weight in and out, keeping a rhythm beat and your stance. Listen for and feel a snap or pop sound on the bag when you hit it. Learn to put your shoulders behind each punch before moving on.

Again, do not let the bag move around. This time let's work on the combinations that you have learned in chapter 4 and appling all the rolling of your hands and crisscrossing each other.

Create a momentum, rhythm and speed. Practice throwing each combination five times each to get a feeling for them before working on the next set of punch combinations. This drill will help you with your speed and take off of the punches, and hit your challenger with combiation punches. Sharp shoot everything to the "X" a first.

Jab, Jab, Cross

| JAB | JAB | CROSS |

Jab, Cross, Lead Hook

| JAB | CROSS | HOOK |

Jab, Lead Hook, Cross

JAB   HOOK   CROSS

Jab, Uppercut, Lead Hook, Cross

JAB   UPPERCUT   HOOK

CROSS

There is one punch that has not been mentioned yet, it is an advance technique. The **Over hand punch** is used to go over your challenger's hands in an arcing motion. It resembles a hook but arcing down as it strikes. It's a Bomb of a punch!

It works great in a combination starting with a lead uppercut going up and then coming down with the overhand with the other hand. Notice where the other hand is that is not punching. This combination is used rarely in a boxer style of a long distance attacks.

Lead Uppercut, Rear Overhand, Lead Hook, Cross

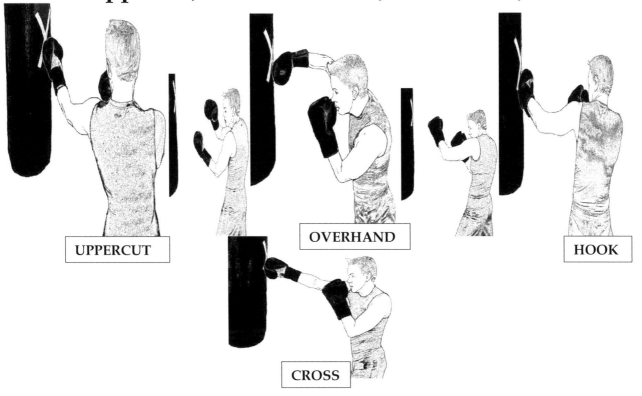

UPPERCUT

OVERHAND

HOOK

CROSS

Jab, Jab, Body Hook, Lead Body Hook, Lead Head Hook

JAB

JAB

HOOK

HOOK

HOOK

Rolling your Uppercuts

Trainer's Tips.

I learned about in-close fighting when I trained my first World Champion, Ada Velez. Her small and compact size allowed her to generated power through her lower half. I always used my long range, shoulder to snap or pop. I practiced having a good boxer's style. Both the boxer and fighter use different methods in their approach. It is important to understand both styles and how to generate the power in the punch using either the shoulder or the butt. The uppercut/hook bag helps to practice using the lower torso (butt) to get the feeling of the power in the punch.

Still using the "**X**" on the bag at eye level and keep yourself in front of it which represents your challenger. Strike your punches on the "**X**", moving with the bag as it moves around. Be sure you bring your punches back as fast as you can on the center line. Do **not** hold the bag out unless you need to measure the distance. **Don't let the bag crowd you.** This is when the bag can get tricky because of the distance and movement along with everything else you have learned. Practice your combinations and six punches. Keep the bag at arm's distance, step in when you punch and back when you are done. Make sure to keep your fighting position. Use your movement with your feet as shown to you on the four cones, tire and circling in previous chapters. Combine everything you have learned so far in this book and put it into play while keeping up with boxing the bag.

Combine what was shown to you on the 4 cones, tire and circling shown in Chapter 3. Put all you have learned from the beginning of this book in to play keeping up with boxing the bag.

In the corner

Keeping your challenger at a long distance and make them reach for you, so they are not as strong. Two different methods were shown to hit the bag to preparation your body for this style.

Remember when hitting the bags:

1. Rip or snap/pop your punches on the bag. The Speed of the punch traveling to the target with each hand.
   .

2. Hit at the end of your punches at longest range.

3. The body weight is shifted forward to the front leg at the peak of the punch when it hits the target getting power from your shoulder and the turn of the fist.

4. Accuracy of your aiming your punch at the target without losing eye focus. Focus on one spot to see all around the center line. Impact should be with the whole fist but the focus on the two front knuckles.

5. Keep a rhythm or pace to a beat.

6. Move, step and slide with proper body positioning and balance on the bag work.

7. Make sure everyone on your team (body) all as a job assignment and work in all you have learned so far. Stay in control.

Short Distance Heavy Bag Training

Power Punching **1**

In Close Fighter's Bag... **2**

In boxing, there is a boxer or the fighter style. You worked in the last chapter on the boxer style and learned to keep a long reach on your challenger. What happens if you are the shorter of the two or you are in-close?   This chapter will introduce two methods in throwing a punch in-close, and generating power with the butt, torso, hips and being seated with the legs behind the punch, instead of the shoulders. This is more a fighter style since you are in the pocket, close, and roughing it up with your challenger.

Turning and rolling with the body to generate Power Punches

The Uppercut/Hook bag helps teach you to generate in-close power punches. If you don't have an uppercut/ hook bag, practice with a heavy bag raised to hip level. The power of the punch is generated by the turning, rolling and swing the body. Imagine swinging a baseball bat to hit the home run with your punch. Make a hard fist and turn the hands inward to you a little to shorten your range before throwing them. This gives more power also. There are two levels to hit your punch with high to the chin or low to the body.

In this drill you must make a tight fist, by rolling your finger into your palm, turning your wrist inward and tightening your pinky finger to lock your wrist tight. The elbow is kept bent, staying behind the fist in a circular motion with the punch like the uppercut or hook punch being shown in illustration below.

Your elbows are close to your hips, keeping your arms up in the body zone, turning to the side as you squat down low with the body, and then coming up in twisting and rolling movement with the punch. Hook your hand inward on contact keeping an arch in the arm and adding additional power to the punch.

Drill 1

Roll your body with the **uppercuts** side to side keeping your fighting stance.
Get a swing like you are swinging a baseball bat keeping your elbows and arms in
your body zone. Be awere of what the other hand is doing as you roll from side to
side switching guard positions and height staying on the center line.

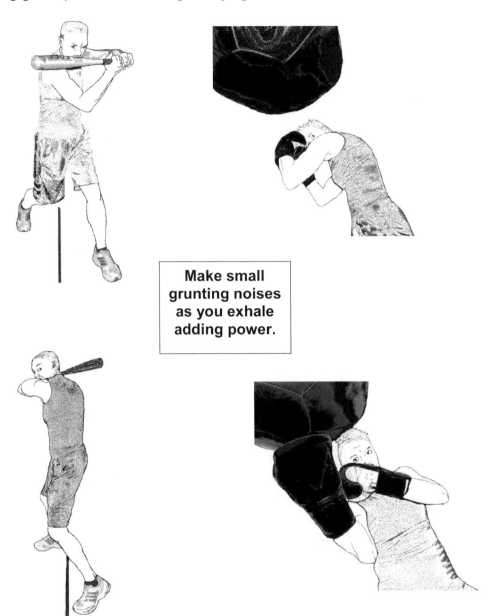

**Make small
grunting noises
as you exhale
adding power.**

76

Throwing with the same motion, add in the **hooks**. As you twist to one side, the hand that is not punching serves as guard as you set up the other hand to thrown a lead hook. When the hook hits the bag roll the punch over to the other side of the bag turning your whole body with the motion in a defensive guard. This is setting you up to throw your other Hook with the other hand. With each punch you want to blow your air out through your mouth to gain the maximum power of the punch. Keep your stance low, knees bent and stay tight and small. Once your hook hits the bag, turn the hook turn back into your body zone.

Throw singles, doubles and triples with the same hand or alternating hands.
Anymore and the power weakens.

Throw a double punch with the same hand.

Shift   Punch   Shift back to same side   Punch

Upper Cut   **Hook**

Once you are done punching keep the rolling motion from side to side. This makes you a harder target to hit. Make a tight fist when generating power and keep your arms tight in your body zone. Try rolling two times then throw you punch.

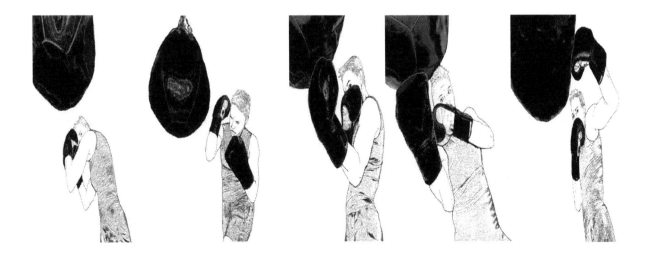

This keeps you unpredictable, gives you the momentum to rest and gets you into a defense and offensive position while you set up for your next attack.

The Fighter's Bag

This is in-close fighting but more of a brawling tactic. It is completely the opposite a boxer's style. Do not lean your head forward. Sit back in your stance to leave room for your arms to stay nice and high between you and the bag or challenger. Your arms are in a guard position using your forearm and fist as a shield, pinching your fists together. Lift your shoulder to your chin to keep tucked and tight to give a smaller body zone with your arms.

Drill 4

One or both arms are in contact with the bag at all times. This contact is used to feel the challenger and your defense. Keep pressure and push the bag out a little.

Throw four to six punches alternating hands. Be fast and slow to alternate the power. Alternating power in the punch keeps the challenger unable to predict your power until it lands..

Work yourself around the bag staying in contact distance with your forearms on the bag. You always want to keep your challenger off balance by moving toward the rear (back) of them in a small circle. This will make your challenger weak and off balance. Hit solid with the whole fist. Sinking into the bag at the center point of impact is your two knuckles. Put a little twist on the fist and elbows when you make contact. Rise up a little with your body to generate power. The punches are not at full range like the boxer but half range out.

Remember always remain tight with your arms in front of you when you are on this bag.

In the corner

No need to cock your arm back to gain power because you use the movement of your body to cock it back in a denfensive move to begin an offensive attack. Stay tight in your body zone and use your body positioning with your arms in guard to help provide the body power behind the punch. This is something you must study and practice. Be creative, imagine you are playing the role of the fighter on the bags. Bags don't think or hit back, so stay in control with your techniues before mixing styles together. Get comfortable with both methods of long to short range.

<u>Timing and Speed Bag Work</u>

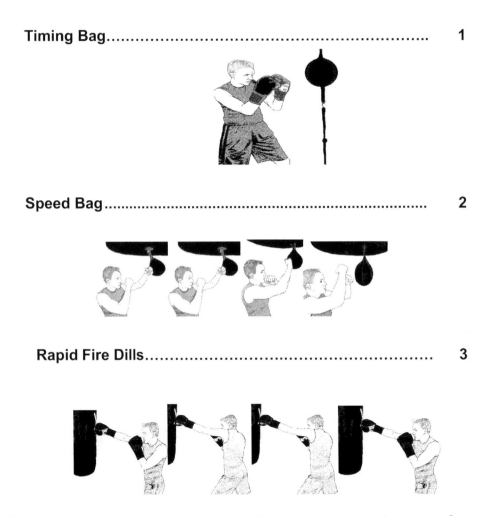

The exercises in this chapter help you build up your reactions, eye focus, timing, speed, endurance and will make your boxing ablities better.

Practice with a double ended bag or a focus bag. If you cannot find one make one. Use a soccer ball tied up in a basketball net with bungee cords.

Stand in front in your fighting stance, hands pinched together in front of your face. Your hands are a little out in front of your face. Hit the bag to work your timing and focus. Don't cock your hands back all the way. Bring them back to the pinching position and stay tight. Once you feel you can hit it the bag in a rhythm work in the six punches while circling the bag. Practice with the two ranges, long and close. This is an excellent bag to work your eye focus, reaction, speed and timing.

Drill 2

Work the speed bag. This helps develop a rolling with your hands. When one goes to hit, the other hand comes underneath the punch that is going out to hit the speed bag. This is a rolling motion repeating itself over again and faster, hitting with the back two knuckles.

Start by hitting with the outside part of the first.

Once you get the rolling down turn your hand over and hit with the front two knuckles. Hit on the same spot on the speed bag. Let it hit the back board coming to the front board and hit it again.

Now twice with one hand then the other one.

Hit the bag with one hand ten times then the other hand.
Get a rhythm, then alternate hands keeping the rhythm while switching.

The harder you hit the bag the faster it will go. When you hit with the right hand you turn your right shoulder in focusing with your right eye and vice versa on the left side.

Rapid fire punching drills

This is a burn out punching drill to help develop your punch and muscle endurance.

Stand in front of the bag and throw 50 fast and hard jabs.

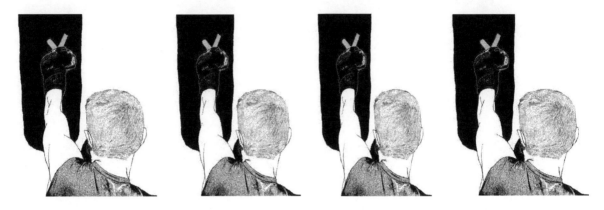

Now rapidly throw a jab and cross alternating fifty times **without breaking rhythm.**
The jab and cross is counted as one.

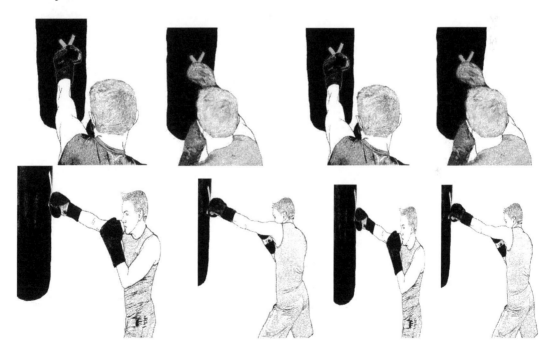

Throw the uppercuts in rapid fire the same way. Remember to keep the elbows in front of the body and punch low. Keep palms up in this drill.

Drill 5

Throw a double hook going low, dipping down to hit. Then with a small twist back, coming up high with the second hook with the same hand then alternate to the other side. Lean over to the same side of the bag you are going to hit when you throw the hook. Turn your body inward with the punch. Do this thirty times on each side.

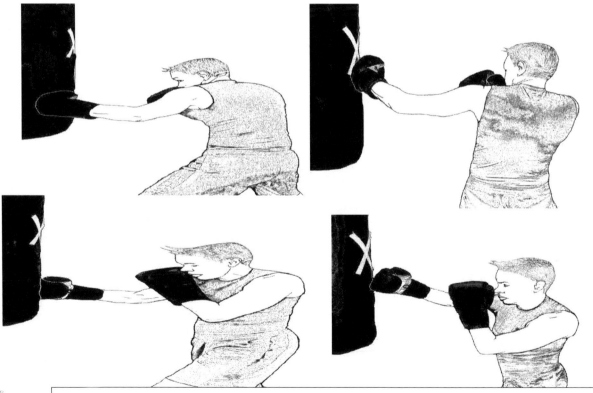

These drills help to prevent muscle fatigue and increase your ability to respond quickly with your eyes, brain and muscles.

Water Break - ROUND OFF

What not to do before fights and long trips.

When you fight, you are there for business only. After the fight nothing matters but before you need to be smart. Rest and get ready mentally. My first Title fight in 1987 with Lucia Ricker (18-0 18 K0s) was also my first time overseas. I was so excited to see another Country, but I did not know how to prepare myself for time change. Holland was 7 hours ahead. I went with my trainer Bert Rodriguez, his wife Karen and my good friend training partner Terry Vargas. Terry introduced me to Bert. Bert, at the time didn't take or train any woman and did not allow women's to step in training area.. But, four years later we landed in Holland for my first title fight. Our excitement for sight-seeing overwhelmed us. We were in walking distance to the Red Light District. Food was on everyone's mind, since we arrived in the morning not eating or sleeping on the plane. By 6 pm we found ourselves sleeping. I woke up at 10:30 with the sun in my eyes and the sound of people on the streets. I sprung out of bed and woke the whole room to get ready for breakfast. As we left the apartment dusk came and we found out it was night time, not morning. Next morning we rented a car to explore Holland since we had four days before the kickboxing fight. We trained outside during evening since we had 18 hours of day light when to train wasn't an issue. The driving got stressful because none of us could read the street signs which were in Dutch and we ended up lost a bunch of times. The next day was weigh-in at the gym my challenger Lucia Ricker trained in. Weigh-in started and I couldn't understand what the commissions were saying since Dutch is their primary language. The weigh-in was in metrics and not in pounds and I didn't know the conversion difference. But, I was underweight from the start, taking the fight at 115 pounds. I tried to gain some weight, getting to121 pounds. The fight was contracted at 127 pounds. I decided I was going to weigh-in with a couple of fish weights in my pockets since I was under and didn't want to get denied the Championship Belt. I stepped on to the scale and it passed the contract weight. I don't by how much on the metric scale. I got off the scale and excused myself to go to the bathroom. I unload all the fish weights in my pants. I returned to step back on the scale. I didn't know how much weighed I lost but I knew I made weight by commissioner's face which looked a little shocked. I couldn't understand so it didn't matter. After the weigh-in, off we went to Germany. It was close to Holland and I wanted to have Lunch at a restaurant on the Shrine. We got back in the evening. I stayed in and rested since the fight was the next day. I was cocky being 9-0 and thought I was the badest woman out there. But when Fight night came, I had a stomach pain, was tired from the trip and lazy. I shook it off. But when we go to the stadium all I wanted to do was sit in the audience and not a piece of lion's meat as the main show. Of course I had to fight, but it was an experience that I will never want to feel again. I lost but gained the respect of the crowd to last the duration against a bigger, stronger, tougher and more experienced fighter like Lucia Ricker. To this day, I make sure my fighters get plenty of sleep right after a long flight, no traveling around to sightsee until after the fight. Check time differences, climate, attitude, culture and type of foods available.

5 Defensive Basic Guard Positions

5 Basic Defensive Positions

Your hands and arms to have a strong, firm position when in guard for incoming attacks. These guards should be used during, before and after an attack when in contact range between you and your challenger.

Always start out in your fighting stance. Blocks are guards done with your forearms or hands with the body in position. Some are done at the same time to leave a hand free to attack. Blocks are done in a zone for target. Your arms are within your body zone and your head never passes over your knee.

Pinching - Standing in front of your challenger when they are throwing straight attacks at you. Pinch your arms together slanting them out on a 45 degree angle for structure. Your fists are touching each other and are at eye level. You are hiding your head behind your arms. Now, crunch your body a little and stay solid in your stance. Remember two arms are better than one. When pinching make tight fists and hold your arms up strong.

Practice switching from an offensive fighting stance and go into a pinch, then back to the fighting stance. Repeat it a few times so you can start to feel it.

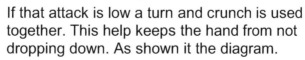

Inward Guards - Are user for a high or low attacks. Your palm, forearm to your elbow is used in this block. You will turn the body inward at the same time.

If that attack is low a turn and crunch is used together. This help keeps the hand from not dropping down. As shown it the diagram.

For a high attack to your head, move a little to the outside, hiding behind your hand from the palm to forearm blocking to the inside. These blocks are used with straight punches like a jab or cross, but can be used for circle attacks like hooks but with some adjustments.

Note: Blocks should stay within your body zone.

Outward Guards - can also be used in two ways; a high attack or a low attack.

Normally the attack is coming from the outside of your body zone, around the side. A body turn, a light crunch and a brush off, or a jamming of the punch up. Like a hook.

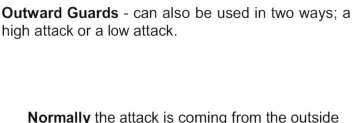

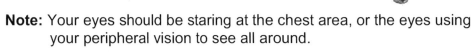

Note: Your eyes should be staring at the chest area, or the eyes using your peripheral vision to see all around.

Upward Guards – are used for high attacks and can be used as an offensive pressing move when going in on your challenger. Use your fist, forearm to your elbow in an upward motion and crunching your body with a slight turn, hiding underneath your arm, looking under your arm.

Note: The other arm is guarding the open areas on the center line between you and your challenger.

Downward Guards – One hand is high covering the head and the other hand is low blocking down low across the body. Crunch down into the strike or a roll away from the strike. Use the down to protect the lower body.

Note: Both arms should be covering your center line in this position. You do not want to fight or start in this blocking position, because in this position your offensive strikes are at a minimum.

In the corner

So far you have learned some blocks to protect yourself from incoming strikes using certain parts of your body's arms. **Always** use these blocks in your shadow boxing and bag work. Add them before going in and after your punch. Flow back and forth from a guard position to a strike in your fighting stance. **Always** return to your fighting position as soon as your block is over. It will and can change quickly. In the next chapter you will use these during, before and after to recover back to your fighting position.

Five years into the fighting game I met my trainer Bert Rodriguez, who started his career in 1962. He taught me the understanding of the center line. I practiced drills over and over again to train my body to guard the center line. It wasn't until I studied Tai-Chi that I understood the use of the center line by moving slowly and gracefully. I learned to ride my hands along the line and my feet positioning. This gave me the ability to feel the center of the balance within me.

Bert and I did a lot of knife throwing and bow and arrow practice where aiming is important. We would even aim the arrows at each other shoot from one center line to the other's center line. We would step to the side when the arrow approached and practice catching it with one hand on the center line. The center line training helped me to stay focused during my fights and made me learn to adjust my center line between myself and my challenger.

Knowing and understanding the center line is an important key to success.

<u>Defensive Training Aides</u>

These are training aides to help practice your defensive movements.

Side to Side Bag

A small filled bag or sock filled with rice, beans or sand hanging down on a string to the bottom of the bag is your shoulder level. The bag represents a straight incoming punch to the head from your challenger. Move your head and shoulder over to the outside to avoid the incoming punch like Jabs or a Cross.

You **must** understand and practice to its fullest, because in **Volume 2,** I will introduce this drill again and will be adding on more material, with techniques and skills.

This is called **slipping** a jab or cross punch, a straight strike. There are two ways in how to slip with the shoulders flipping. Let's practice with the side to side bag.

Note: The side to side bag should never get behind your head in the beginning.

Start out standing in front of the side to side bag; **do not** let the bag move yet. Move from your center line by shifting your head, shoulder and body weight to the side, towards the outside of challenger's punch, the bag. Do not step with your feet at first, just adjust your feet by swifting and pivoting to keep your balance

Move your head side to side while you are in balance with your body and one hand is between your face and the bag in an inward guard. Keep your eyesight on the middle of the imaginary line drawn in your head of the challenger on the back side of the bag. The bag is the punch. Practice shifting your weight, flipping the shoulder to the inside and over from side to side without the bag moving. Once you feel the balance and you're shifting, you can move on the next drill.

Drill 2

Move your head over to the right as you throw your left jab. Your lead hand is underneath the side to side bag on that imaginiary center line, then to the other side with the cross.

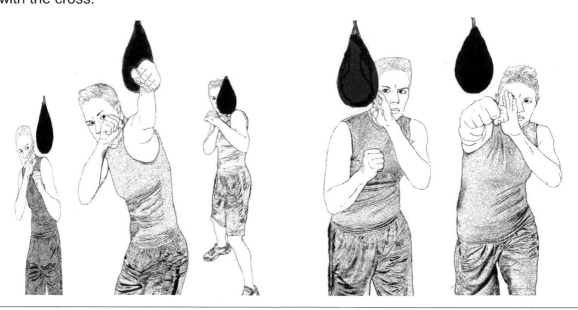

Note: The head will start the movement before the punch, throw directly under the bag.

Drill 3

Add your outward high blocks to Drill 2.

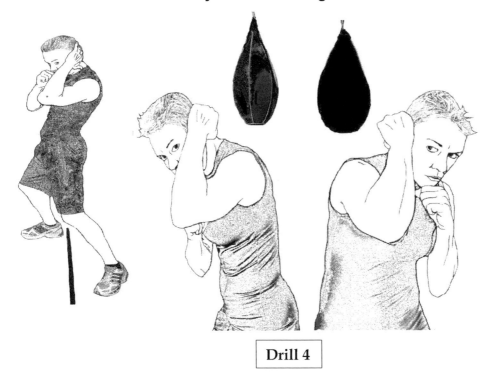

Drill 4

Now the Hook

Twist your body from side to side and throw on the center line with the hook underneath the bag turning the punch into you. The other hand on guard as you roll your body with the strike.

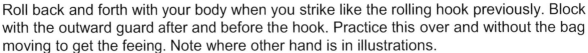Roll back and forth with your body when you strike like the rolling hook previously. Block with the outward guard after and before the hook. Practice this over and without the bag moving to get the feeing. Note where other hand is in illustrations.

Shifting over to the left side, this time flipping both shoulder to the outside of the bag and throwing an uppercut with the lead hand turning your body with the punch to the center line behind the bag. Shift over to the right and throw the rear uppercut as you turn your body inward toward the on the center line aiming up at the challenger's chin. Practice throwing your longest range to feel the full movement and balance of the punch. Practice this drill at first without the bag moving.

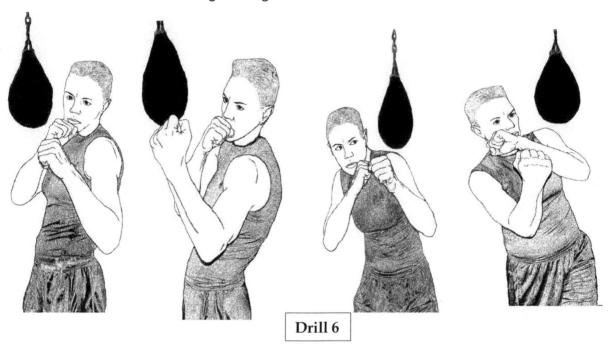

Drill 6

Now push the bag out and let it swing back and forth it is simulating a straight a punch being thrown at your head. Time it, slip it at the last second and throw a punch. Make sure you are in balance all through the strike and slipping. You might need to take a small adjustment step to the side with your left foot going to left side or the right to right side, but only one foot will step not both. The other foot stays as your stability foot.

Practice all six punches and never let the bag get behind you.

Ducking is when your challenger is throwing any attack high to the head. It is used to avoid a circular motion strike resembling a hook. Imagine a baseball bat is swinging at your head and you duck down to get out of the way.

Placing a rope straight across two poles by attaching both ends in a straight line, the rope should be shoulder height. The rope represents your challenger's incoming punch. The rope doesn't move so you are going to duck down on one side and weave over to the other side with your head and body. Stand in front of the rope in your fighting stance. Practice ducking down first, then a little step with the right foot over to the side and back a little as you weave over, coming up to the other side with an outward high guard. Duck to the other side as you step forward a little to that side with your left foot at a time like an inch worm. Duck by bending your knees. You learned the stepping with the four cones drill. Practice the ducking over to the other side as you weave your head to that side. Keep your fighting stance and do an outward high guard when you rise up. Get the feeling and balance before moving to the next drill.

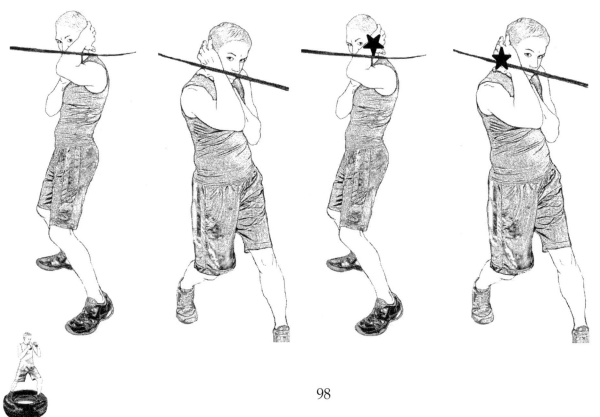

Drill 8

Duck under stepping back with the outside guard and turning your body slightly to the side away from the rope as you block. Twist back in and throw a cross punch with the opposite hand over the rope. The other hand is still in a guard but turns in on the outside catching the punch you and the rope.

Note: The hands turn into the catching hand when you are punching with the other one. Make sure your body is working together.

Try both sides. Practice on repetition. Start out doing it 20 times. Each side is counted as 1, before moving on.

Once you feel you have the idea of throwing one punch add three punches over the rope after ducking over to the other side.

Always practice keeping your fighting position during your movements down and over, remembering the hand that isn't punching is on your center line between you and the rope on guard.

Practice the twist of the body to get your full range with each punch. This will not only give you a longer ranger, but also power in the punch and a better defensive position. Repeat this drill until you get the feel and groove of it.

Note: The hand that is not throwing is in a defensive guard before, after and during.

I am a picky trainer having my boxer's hands on the center line when they throw a punch. I got tired and lazy one year fighting with some of them to keep their hands up. Most of them were copying pictures of other professional boxers who have their lead hand low and the other hand on the side of their face. There was a fight in which my boxer was winning with ease and had just thrown a punch. The other hand was up but to the side of his face like the pictures, not on the center line. The challenger threw a punch at the same time and found the open center line on my boxer and dropped him. I warn not to practice that bad habit with that hand to the side of the face, but on the center line between you and your challenger to only use the hand on the side as your face as a guard or block when it's called for, like in these drills.

Bobbing and Weaving

Bobbing and weaving is usually done by the small fighter when boxing a taller figher. The smaller fighter stays low making an even smaller target when coming into close range. The upper body is going from one side to other of your challenger center line in a bobbing movement, staying low. Great movement to use when your challenger is tall and throwing a high straight attack like a jab or cross. You are staying low underneath your challenger's arms.

I was outclassing and winning in two fights with ease. I was getting cocky thinking I was invisible and that I was going to knock out my challenger, but it almost turned the other way around. I was almost the one to get knocked out. Never think you have it until it is over. I have almost been knockout twice in my career but because I was a good bluffer, I knew how to tie up my challenger until I could get my senses together. Both times I had the momentum going in the fights. I was winning and I was going to knock them out. That arrogant thinking made me take a shot that almost made me lose the fight. The good thing I was in great condition and was able to recover quickly and come back to win both of the fights.

Practicing with the rope, squat down and bobb and weave three times from one side over to the other side, not coming up all the way, on the third weave come up to get your balance and postion. Once that feels good, do the same thing except when you come up throw three punches over the rope.

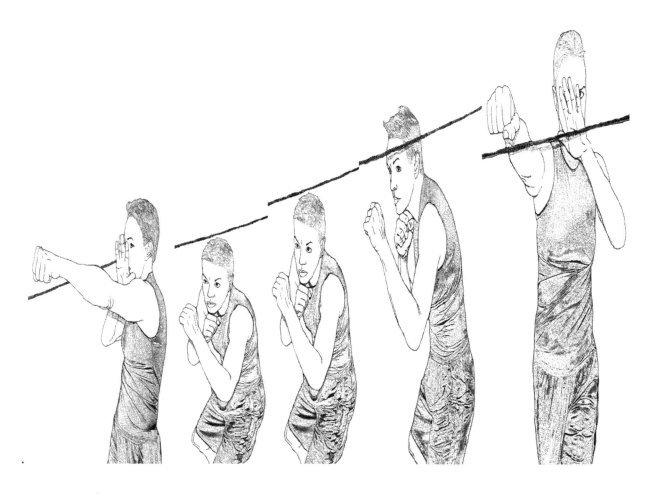

In the corner

Side to side is normally done when slipping a jab or a cross or any straight strike high to the head. The rope resembles an attack coming in high, usually from the side of you like a hook for ducking.

The set of illustrations below shows the two opposite sides of the rope with the right and left punch. Same with the Side to Side bag. Always working toward the back of your challenger.

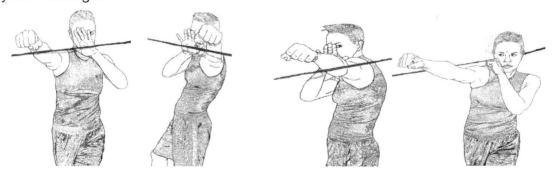

Put all the chapters together and study the postions of your whole body with good habits. In the next book (the Mind) these drills will play a large role in advancing to your next level in boxing and fighting.

Wrapping The Hand

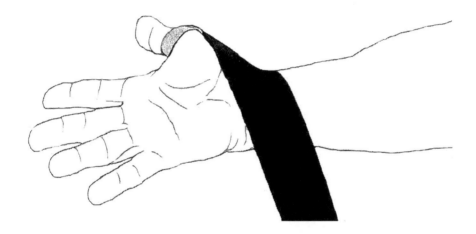

Hand wraps give extra support to your wrists and hands. They keep the wrist aligned and pad the knuckles when making contact to prevent breakage

The size of length of hand wraps vary and should be determined by how big you are. Most boxers use the longest length wraps.

Your boxing gloves will have a little padding to protect your knuckles when you are hitting. The harder you hit the more padding you need to protect the hand. 14oz or 16oz gloves are mostly used for gloves unless you are a Heavyweight or a Heavy hitter then use18oz or 20oz

Place the thumb loop over thumb and start at the wrist. Keep your hand straight, firm and spread wide.

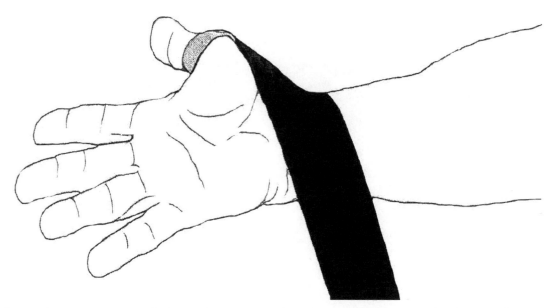

Start the wrap around the wrist going toward your elbow, overlaying each wrap over the wrap going up around 3 and then around down 2 towards the wrist.

NOTE: Do not wrap the hand wrap to tight. Just lay it on and tighten it up on the final stretch. Your hand will pump up bigger, like muscles when you start punching with the hand.

Go around your hand 3 times.

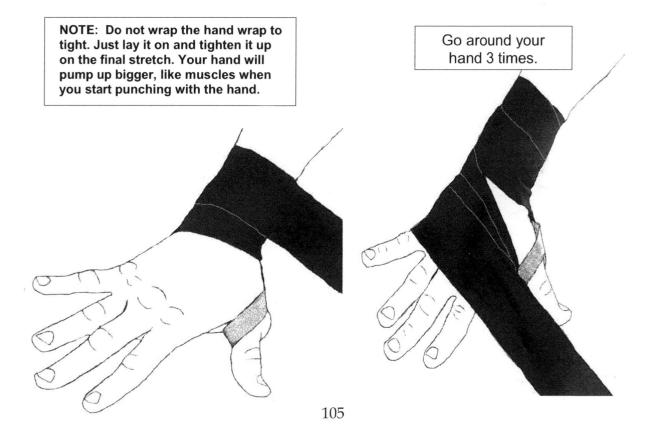

Make a cushion by folding the wrap two or three times on the top of your hand going only over all the knuckles

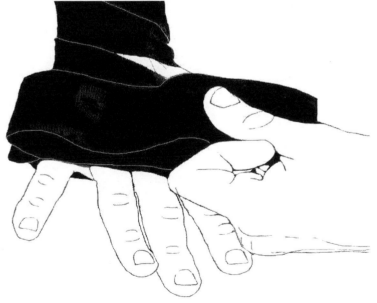

Finish the padding you made by the index finger.

Wrap it one more time around to secure padding.

Flip your hand over.

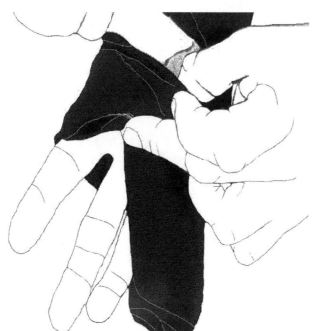

Loop underneath the wrap around the hand on the palm side of the hand from the top.

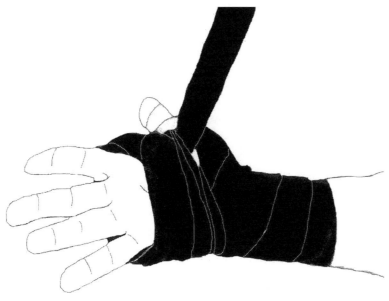

Bring the wrap. All the way through. Pull up.

Now bring the wrap between the index and middle finger, turning your hand back over.

108

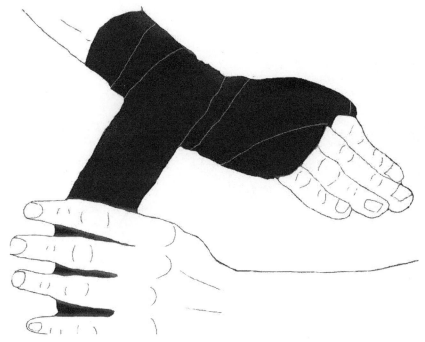

Pull the wrap down to the wrist by the thumb. Make sure you make a fist to check to see it is not to tight.

Wrap around the wrist twice.

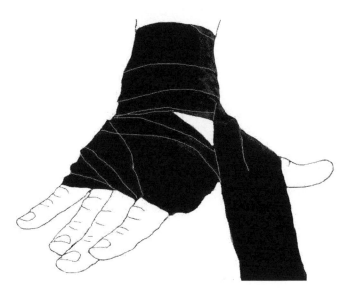

Wrap thumb. Go a complete full wrap around the thumb and come on top of the wrist.

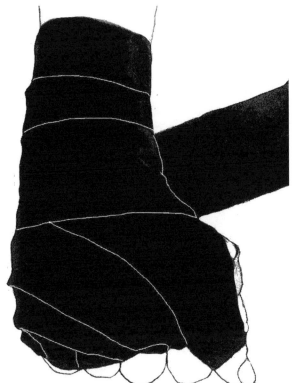

Continue a full wrap around the wrist.

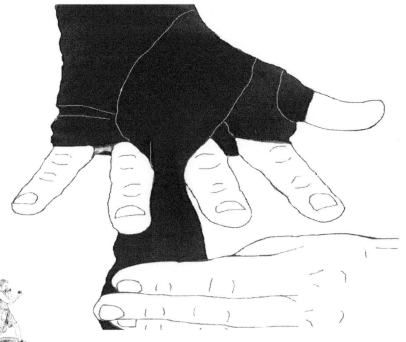

Bring the wrap up and through the middle finger.

110

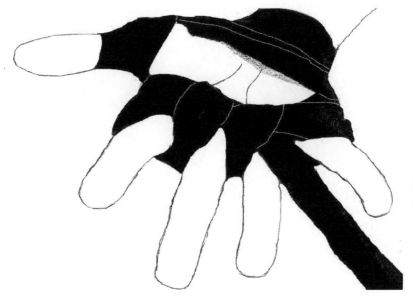

Flip your palm over and loop the wrap over and under

Pull it out and tighten the bar you are making on your hand wrap.

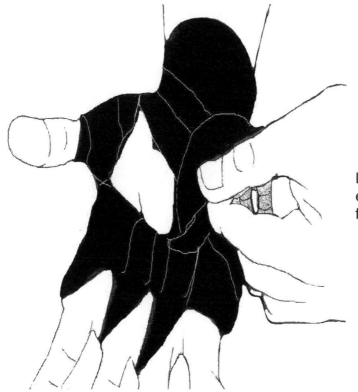

Loop it again going toward the end of the hand near your pinky finger.

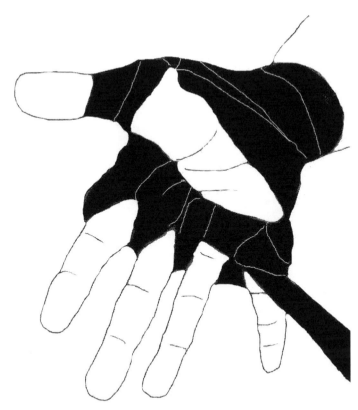

Pull through the pinky up to the other side of the hand.

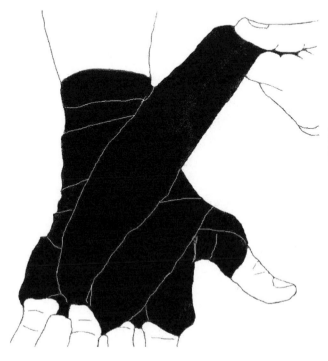

Bring the wrap over the top of your hand towards the thumb.

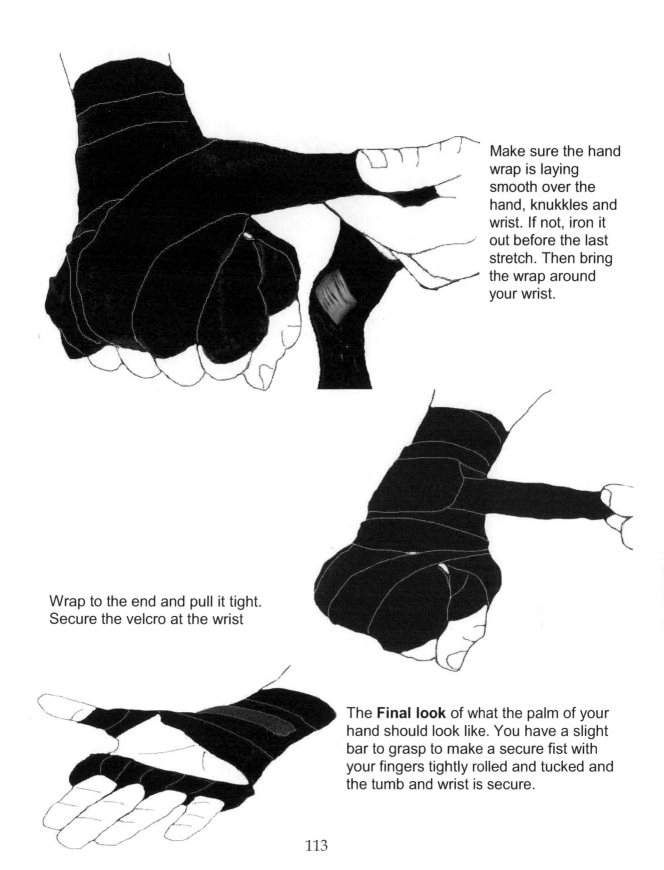

Make sure the hand wrap is laying smooth over the hand, knukkles and wrist. If not, iron it out before the last stretch. Then bring the wrap around your wrist.

Wrap to the end and pull it tight. Secure the velcro at the wrist

The **Final look** of what the palm of your hand should look like. You have a slight bar to grasp to make a secure fist with your fingers tightly rolled and tucked and the tumb and wrist is secure.

113

In the corner

Everyone has a prefereance to put on their handwraps on, this is just one of many ways.

I've seen good boxers practice without making a fist because it makes them feel faster by keeping an open hand throwing a punch. However, when making hard contact they end up breaking or hurting their hands and wondering why. It is a bad habit in fighters. They see other fighter's and copy them shadow boxing. Making a good, tight fist helped me not injure my hands throughout my years. It also gave me hands of stone. So when I wanted to hit hard I had a strong fist with intensity behind it. A tight fist gave me power. I was able to throw a one inch punch with a turn at the end to land it solid. This helped me understand that the way we practice it is the way it will come out. Practice good habits. You will not have time to fix them when you need them.

In association with

WIBF
WOMEN'S INTERNATIONAL BOXING FEDERATION, INC.

ALADDIN
HOTEL & CASINO · LAS VEGAS

AND SANCTIONED BY THE NEVADA STATE ATHLETIC COMMISSION

PROUDLY PRESENTS

THE BOXING EVENT OF THE YEAR !!!

WOMEN'S WORLD CHAMPIONSHIP BOXING

SIX WORLD TITLES

REGINA HALMICH GERMANY	WORLD SUPER FLYWEIGHT TITLE 112 LBS	YVONNE TREVINO USA
BRIDGET RILEY USA	WORLD BANTAMWEIGHT TITLE 118 LBS	FIENIE KLEE HOLLAND
BONNIE CANINO USA	WORLD FEATHERWEIGHT TITLE 124 LBS	DELIA GONZALEZ USA
DEIRDRE GOGARTY IRELAND	WORLD LIGHTWEIGHT TITLE 130 LBS	LAURA SERRANO MEXICO
DANIELLA SOMERS BELGIUM	WORLD SUPERLIGHTWEIGHT TITLE 136 LBS	HELGA RISOY NORWAY
MARY ANN ALMAGAR USA	WORLD SUPERWELTERWEIGHT TITLE 149 LBS	DEIRDRE NELSON N. IRELAND

FIRST FEMALE FISTIC SUPERSHOW !!!

APRIL 20TH 1995 7:30 P.M.

TICKETMASTER

ALADDIN

This was the First Sanctioning Body in the history of boxing to give World Title to women. These were the best female boxers in the World then. I was honored and humbled to be a part of this historic event.

Getting Started
A Workout Routine

Chapter **11**

116

Round Bell

Practice with a round bell or a stop watch that can keep time intervals for you.

Rounds are two or three minutes intervals with a thirty second or one minute break between rounds. Decide how many rounds you want to complete in your session before you start and finish those rounds.

Start out with rounds on the 2 minutes intervals and then move to three.

The reasoning behind round work is maintaining the mental focus. Train yourself to stay aware and focused for the round. Have tunnel vision and do not let anything distract you.

The conditioning is training the body to fighting. Teaching it not to be lazy and to give quality of action instead of waiting, thinking you have time.

You will need an open area
1. **heavy bag**
2. **double ended bag**
3. **speed bag**
4. **jump rope**
5. **hand wraps**
6. **bell timer**
7. **boxing gloves to complete a basic boxing workout routine**

The warm up drills to follow are for 4 – 5 rounds of boxing.
Increase the rounds as your cardio increases.

This is a four, three minute with thirty second break round drill. Conditioning is the most important thing in boxing. You will need to move to get out of the way of an attack. If you cannot move out of the way of you will get hit.

Round 1: Jumping Rope.

Don't worry what pace. As you get in better shape, your beat will get quicker. This warms up foot work, your cardio, coordination, rhythm, and boxer's bounce.

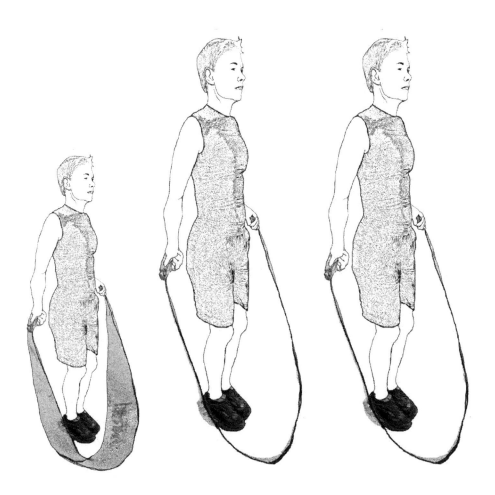

Round 2: Calisthenics Exercises

Jump right into doing some calisthenics exercises, these are call plyometric when you will do a series of 30 second intervals then move to the next exercise changing the pace, the beat and the intensity from power to speed. This requires cardio and endurance by quickly changing the momentum with no upset. It is a good jump start to getting and making sure you are in shape (heart and wind).

Start right away during the 30 second break, for 3 ½ minutes long round.

Start during the rest period with **Push-ups** for 30 seconds. It doesn't matter how many you do just don't stop for the 30 seconds.

Go right into **Mountain Climbers** for 30 seconds. Bring your knees to up to your chest into a steady rhythm like climbing alternating your legs.

120

Do Mountain Jacks for the next 30 seconds. Start out by stretching out long in a push-up position. Jump forward with both feet together keep your hands low. Tap or hit your stomach with both hand for form. Look up and spring up with a jump into the air with both feet as you stretch your arms up toward the ceiling. Land down with both feet, tap or hit your stomach again then crouch down bring your hands to the floor by your feet and stretch back out into g push-up position with a hop.

121

The next 30 seconds, Run quickly in place with your feet spread wide like hitting the speed bag . Move your feet with your hands working on speed. Your hands are moving, rolling past each other at eye level keeping a rhythm with your hands and feet.

Your feet move up and down rapidly.

122

Next, Superman Jumps for 30 seconds. Squat down and bring your hands up with your thumbs touching your temples. Jump up with both feet into the air as you push downward with your hands this helps you to get a better spring up and keep good form.

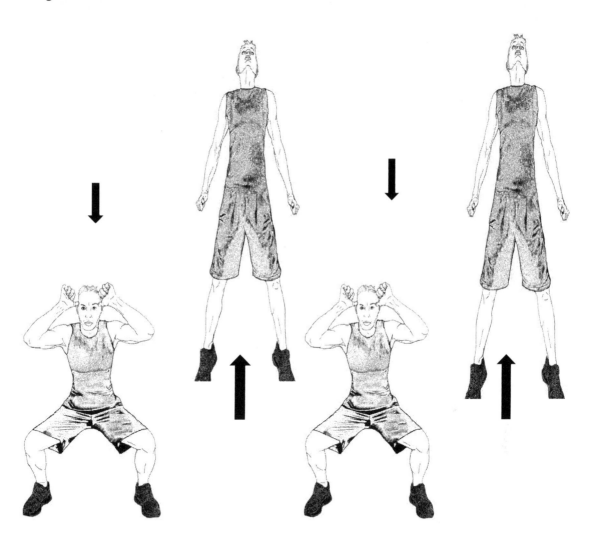

Thirty seconds of Jumping Jacks, bring your arms straight up from the side and then straight up to the front alternating from side to front for 30 seconds.

124

Last thirty seconds of the round do Knee Raises have your hands interlock on the back of your neck and raise your knee to the opposite side of your chest and elbow. Alternate from right to left with a bounce and crunch each side.

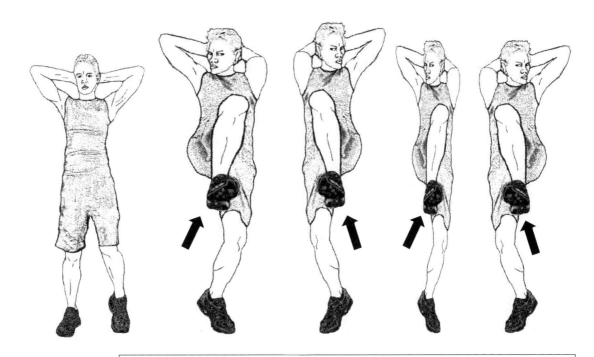

Finish. Take your 30 second break, before round 3

Round 3

Go back to jumping rope. Now that you are warmed up try different jumps and tricks with the rope (Reference videos on jumping rope). Everyone has their own style. Make sure to jump with intensity. Jump briskly and do not relax as if you were jumping for 30 minutes.

Round 4: **Another round of Plyometrics**- Thirty seconds each

30 Seconds- **Push-ups**

30 Seconds - **Mountain Climbers**

30 Seconds- **Mountain Jacks**

30 Seconds- **Running in place.**

30 Seconds- **Superman Jumps**

30 Seconds- **Jumping Jacks**.

30 Seconds- **Knee Raises**.

Finish. Take your 30 second break, before round 5.

Last and final Round 5 – Jump Rope

Now that you are warmed up with the rope and plyometric. Let's shadow box.

Set the boxing bell or timer for a two minute duration with a 30 second rest at first to stay focus and get in shape. Later you can move to three minute durations, but remember **it's quality instead of quanity that matters**.

**Shadow Boxing
2**

Round 1:

Resistant Bands are good accessory aides to help build up your boxing and keeps you tight.

Shadow box in front of a mirror and image your reflection is the challenger.   Check your form and position of your feet and hands.

Keeping a fighting stance, throw your punches. Your feet stepping with each punch, landing them straight down as in Chapter 3's stomping and stepping exercises.

Throw all six punches at first, without moving your feet. Once you get the hang of it start moving the feet with the hands.

Reference Chapters 1,2,3,4 and 8.

Change them up in different orders except throwing more combinations starting with a Jab, with the lead hand, not letting your challenger anticipate when you are throwing more than one at the same time go through your check list on your body.

1. A tight fist,
2. Eyes are focused
3. Aiming at a target or spot
4. Breathing when punching balance,
5. Your right hand and left hand playing different roles of offense and the other hand is defense in a guard position.

Note: Stay busy throwing punches, but don't rush or go to fast. You will miss the feeling of the move.

Round 2:

Practice shadow boxing on the tire with a rhythmic bounce forward and back. You can add some hand weights if you want to have your arms work a little bit more. First, get into the groove. The rhythm is with the body and legs shifting your body weight to the front leg and shifting to the back leg, as shown in the picture below. Get the flow and pracice your combination punches. (Reference Chapters 1,2,3,4, and 8)

Round 3:

Shadow box around a circle. Place your rope on the floor in a cicle which will represent your challgener.

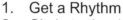

1. Get a Rhythm
2. Circle to the right or the left
3. Step in, and out
4. feet are on the ground when punching –stompin
5. Challenge is on center line.

The rope resemble where your challenger is and should be. Punch to the center line. Have one hand in offense and one hand in defense on the center line. This means that one hand is out a little firther than the other hand. One hand is high and one hand covering the lower part of your body.

Add in your shadow boxing in round 1 and 2 drill. However you are not using accessories or helping tools to do it this time around the circle. Keep a long circle stepping back (out) or forward (in) to the left or to the right, but circling around. Mix it all in. Watch your commitment and do not fall to much forward into the circle.

Make sure that your feet step and slide over without crossing each other.

Round 4:

The Side to Side Bag (Maze Bag). Push the bag out having it swing straight in and out in front of you. Practice like you are boxing/fighting your challenger and slip to the side as you avoid getting hit by a punch (bag) and throwing a block and punches. **Reference Chapter 8.**

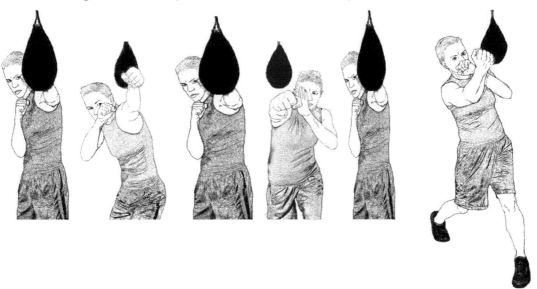

Round 5: Ducking and Dipping. Imagine the rope is the challenge's arm throwing a punch. **Reference Chapter 9**

$$\boxed{\textbf{Bag Training}\\ \textbf{3}}$$

Put on your boxing gloves and start out with your boxing station work out. Set the boxing bell or timer for a 2 minute intravals with a 30 second rest at first to work on staying focused and until you get in shape. Later you can move to 3 minute intravals, but remember it's quality instead of quanity that matters.

Round 1: Double End Bag / Timing Bag. Keep those hands pinched and practice boxing the bag. (Refence Chapter 7)

Round 2: Ripping punches at the Bag. Do not let the bag move freely without a hand on it. Keep it at your longest range. Always go over your check list and know where your team assignments to do to be at your fullest. (Reference Chapter 5.)

Round 3: Box the bag with quick speed. Keep a bounce of in and out, crisscrossing your punches as they roll by each other. This bag is where you work those combinations. (Reference Chapter 5 & Chapter 4)

Example on the shifting that you should have with this drill or in this round when hitting the bag

ROUND 4: Boxing a moving target. The "X" represents your challenger and a place to stay focused during the duration (Reference Chapter 5).

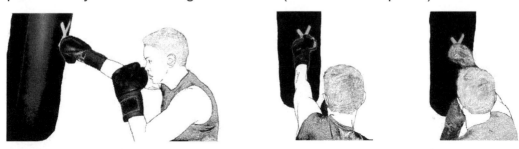

Round 5: Fighting the bag in close putting and the pressure on your challenger. You are controlling your challenger making them uneasy (Chapter 6).

Round 6: Last and final striking round so finish strong, throw power
punches and sitting down with your torso. Pick up power and momentum. Think of Mike
Tyson. (Reference Chapter 6.)

Roll your body all the way over to the other side with the punch or just
for defense and roll over again 2 mores time to get a rolling side to
side shifting affect. This way challenger doesn't know when you are
throwing. Do not be predictable.

Round 7: Push and hold the bag out to work your shoulders and arms to keep your
hands up and strong. (Reference Chapter 5.)

Round 8: Stay on the speed bag a round without missing beat. Change up the
different rhythms. (Reference Chapter 7.)

This concludes the basic workout routine for boxing. It should take no more than one hour long. This routine should be performed at least twice a week. Remember to just practice on your basic without having the timer on and do not rush through everything. The next book will have more boxing/fighting routines to do with some advanced versions of the routines in this book.

> Note: Hold book backwards and flip corner edges of even pages to view combinations in motion

Body, Mind and Soul

BOOK 1 of the TRILOGY

Made in the USA
Charleston, SC
26 June 2013